W9-BAJ-565

UNDERSTANDING BOYS

UNDERSTANDING

by
CLARENCE G. MOSER

BOYS

ASSOCIATION PRESS :: NEW YORK

55
Printed in the United States of America
American Book–Stratford Press, Inc., New York

CONTENTS

UNDERSTANDING BOYS

CHAPTER 1

Understanding a Boy

This is a book about boys, those wonderfully precious, amazingly complex and rather baffling bundles of energy, whose growth is so challenging and rewarding. It is written for all adults who want to understand boys and be helpful to them in their growing up. It is written by one whose years of intimate leadership of boys, shared with the boys themselves, with parents, other adults, and communities, has built a faith in the ability and desire of all of them to play their part in the boy's development. It is written by one who believes that human nature can be trusted, that problem solving is a normal part of growth, and that lack of growth is a perversion of man's nature.

A boy will always present a challenge to adults. To parents he is a part of them, a hope, a dream, a nuisance, a pest. To other adults, he is the promise of the future, the assurance that their achievements will live after them.

As he grows older, he peddles the family secrets until the teacher knows as much about the home as he does. He seems to be his happiest when he is so covered with mud that no one can see where to kiss him; when one needs a moment's rest a boy becomes perpetual motion. He has been described as one who can "swim like a fish, balk like a mule, bellow like a bull, act like a pig, or behave like a jackass, according to climatic conditions."

In adolescence, when it seems that he is about old enough to talk things over, he doesn't consult those with experience, but quotes the "pipsqueak-lamebrain" kid down the block as his authority. Home chores are now performed without the slightest enthusiasm. Home seems to be the place where he expresses his disgust with everything adults try to do for him. Actually, he uses home mostly as the base from which to depart. He is the star boarder who needs a private secretary to keep straight his game schedules and appointments.

How adults actually live with him and love him is amazing, but they do. Despite the showdowns and the flare-ups which are the safety valves in any home, he never gets beyond the family love and community concern. He usually knows it and as long as he feels sure of it, he is free to continue to grow.

Parents are unsung heroes

Parents are the unsung heroes of many communities. Those who throw barbs at them, blaming them for all that happens, rarely see the whole story. They seldom see all the community forces bearing down on the family which make it next to impossible for them to win. Those who complain or sit in righteous judgment seldom picture themselves in the position of the family facing difficulty or feel so moved to do something about it that action results. Monday morning quarterbacking is no more helpful in the family situation than it is for Saturday's football games.

Blaming parents for everything that happens is usually unjustified and rarely helpful; it almost always makes their task more difficult. A few parents do appear to neglect or fight against their children, but such actions are born of being harassed, anxious, or beset by problems beyond their ability. Criticism adds to the problem rather than contributing to the solution. But guiding them to an understanding of their own motivations behind actions and attitudes leading to conflict can provide positive contributions.

Parents need the support of the community in their work with children. As the strengths of a family support those of its members who are weak, so too must the strengths of the community lend support to those families who need help. If there are problem boys in the community, it is a sign of weaknesses in that community. As illness strikes those who are weak and exposes the entire community to danger, so does a problem boy give warning to the community that in some way it has failed to immunize that boy against social failure.

There is no group of people in any community more eager to help boys grow up than their parents. Those who have worked with parents and children over a wide range of cultural and economic levels testify to the eagerness of parents to have their children grow into fine citizens. The few exceptions make the headlines while the others perform their job quietly with all the insight they possess, day after day. Anyone who doubts this needs only to talk with parents about their children, or to observe parents at firsthand in their community.

Perhaps the spirit of all parents is revealed in the story of the father and son at a track meet. The father had been a college star and now, following college, he was running on a city Y.M.C.A. track team. He was a half-miler. Some of his records still stand at the small college where he leaped to fame. A neighboring Y.M.C.A. and the city Y.M.C.A. were engaged in a dual meet. The father had already won his half-mile run but had agreed to pace the opponents in the mile because none of his teammates had arrived for this race. At the start of the race, his eight-year-old son, accompanied by his neighborhood friends, mounted the judges' steps where the contestants would finish. His father was completing his second lap of the quarter-mile track when he began to feel nauseated. He decided to finish his usual half mile and then drop out. Approaching the judges' stand, he saw his son pointing at him. As he passed he heard his son say to his friends, his finger following the pace of his father, "There goes my daddy." The father couldn't stop. He told the judge afterwards, "I'd have finished that race if I had had to crawl the last hundred yards."

That is the spirit of most parents. Those who have worked with children, from the underprivileged to the overprivileged, tell the same story. Fathers and mothers are eager to do the best for their children. The big problem is how to translate the eagerness that is always there into understanding, helpful efforts.

Living with boys is inspiring and rewarding

Living with boys, however, is not all problems. It has its inspirational and rewarding side, too. When the boy is small and depends on those about him, being necessary to him is a source of deep satisfaction. He draws the love and attention he needs from those about him and rewards them with his affection and growth. As he grows older, he takes this care and love for granted, seldom expressing appreciation for it, and he inspires them with his independence and achievements. This is the pattern, generation after generation. The home or community is not truly appreciated until one moves from it. In these days, however, there are some off-guard moments when an adolescent reveals his heart and then quickly conceals it in an embarrassed sort of way. Those occasions are treasures closeted within the family. There are other times when a boy's courage and vision fairly take away one's breath.

It was in the second semester of his senior year in high school that Howard went to his counselor and announced that he was going to go to college in the fall. The counselor listened as he advanced his reasons, but knowing Howard's poor scholastic record, he began to raise the questions which would help the boy see that college for him could be only a doubtful use of time and money. The counselor was thoroughly convinced that Howard was not college material, but he did not want to give the boy that answer; he wanted Howard to discover it for himself. Toward the close of the half-hour interview, Howard was still persistent in his desire to go to college, so the counselor asked where he intended to go. He could hardly believe his ears when he heard the answer, "Harvard." Concealing his amazement as best he could, the counselor asked a few more questions and invited Howard to come back in a few weeks to discuss it again. But Howard did not come back, so the counselor considered the matter closed.

Howard graduated from high school. The counselor closed his file and forgot about him in the rush of other students. Some eight years later, at an alumni open house between Christmas and New Year's, he recognized Howard across the room looking at him. He smiled, but not wanting to embarrass the boy with an "I told you so," he turned to nearby friends and engaged in conversation. The counselor moved from one group of alumni to another, from room to room, and Howard always seemed to be in the room with him. It became evident that a conversation could not be avoided. They met near the punch bowl, exchanged greetings and light conversation, but Howard wouldn't be shaken off. Finally the counselor asked Howard what he was doing, whereupon he got the story. Howard was finishing graduate work in Harvard Business School. He had done his undergraduate work at Harvard and had graduated with honors. He ended by thanking the counselor for his interview while in high school, saying, "If you hadn't been so sure I could not do it, maybe I would not have been so sure I could." The counselor declares he has never undersold a boy since that time.

Gregg was a high school junior from Virginia. A Y.M.C.A. Conference discussion of racial discrimination convinced him that people ought to be valued on the basis of what they are and on what they contribute to life, rather than on factors over which they have no control, such as race or national origin. As a senior, he became president of the Youth Council in his city. Under his leadership the Council became integrated, including representatives of minority groups. At a Spring Conference on a college campus, delegates from all groups gathered for an examination and discussion of democracy. The University opened its Union Building and Field House for the recreation periods in the afternoon and early evenings. One of the guest leaders, strolling around during the recreation period, stepped onto the balcony of the swimming pool. To his surprise, boys and girls of the Conference, including the minority groups, were swimming together and having a wonderful time. Stepping up to Gregg, he expressed the hope that adults in the Community would not hear about this and misunderstand it. Gregg looked him right in the eye and said, "You know, sometimes adults ought to be more like kids." The guest leader told the story that night with deep respect for Gregg and his statement.

A team of junior high school boys was playing for the basketball championship. These boys were almost a United Nations team, mostly from the wrong side of the track. Their uniforms were a variety of hand-me-downs and soiled white shirts. Playing in the big University Field House was too much for them. At the end of the first half of ragged play for them, their opponents had doubled the score. They sat dejectedly in the locker room. The captain called the group together. "We can play better than that. I move we pray." Heads from three religions bowed as the captain asked not that they win the game, but that they play as well as they knew how. The second half was different. Playing as they knew they could, they gained steadily and pulled ahead to win in the last two minutes. But victory is not the point of the story. The captain asked the coach to keep people outside the locker room door for a few minutes after the game, so the team could be alone. Newsmen sensed a story but could not get in. Photographers wanted a picture but they had to wait. It was quiet inside. The boys were not forgetting to say thanks for the strength they had received.

A father decided to surprise the family by driving them to nearby Atlantic City for the week end. The biggest thrill of the trip was the family dinner at a famous restaurant. It was the idea of the twelve-year-old son, who made it his treat to the family of six. The sixteen dollars came from the earnings of his newspaper delivery route.

A seven-year-old and his father raised a little rabbit, feeding it milk from an eye dropper at first. After seven weeks they took it out in the field to set it free. Sitting in the grass, they opened the box and let him hop away. "It's hard to give up something you love, but he wanted to be free, didn't he?" said the lad. His father nodded. He couldn't speak.

This entire book could be filled with stories of inspiration of living with boys. These are enough to illustrate the point.

Human nature can be trusted

The more one studies child development, the more one becomes convinced that human nature can be trusted. There is abundant evidence that the body provides in extreme detail for its physical growth and development. There is increasing evidence that a healthy personality grows naturally and easily and calls forth the type of response that it needs, and it is the very response that those about the boy seem most ready to give him at the time.

Long ago, Harry Emerson Fosdick told the story of the derelict boat sunk in the sand of a tidal basin along the New England coast, which had to be moved for one of the footings of a new bridge that was to be built on that very spot. The engineers used tugs, ballast tanks, sand suckers, and everything they knew, but the derelict stuck fast. Finally, one young engineer proposed that when the tide was out, they anchor four huge scows above the derelict, attach chains between the scows and the derelict, and let the incoming tide pull the derelict from the sand pocket. The chains were attached. On the shore the engineers sat watching as the tide started to rise. The chains grew taut. The mighty Atlantic Ocean continued to roll in. The sand could hold the derelict no longer. She pulled from her long moorings and floated out of the way. To some, this analogy may seem far fetched; but those who co-operate and team with the nature of the person, instead of fighting for their own program, have found the key to the development of a healthy personality in boys. Most of what the boy seeks and needs is natural for adults and those around him to give. It all depends on their ability to read his signals.

Different generations live in different worlds

One of the problems of living with boys and understanding their living is the gap between the generations.

"We lose contact with our children because we do not see where they live," said a parent recently when speaking of her married son who had moved to another state. But the miles between towns is only one distance between children and adults. No two generations live in the same time, though they live in the same year, for their experiences separate them. Even though they face the same problems with the same feelings and needs, the situations are different, for the child lives in a different world within and a new world without. These worlds are so different from those of the older generation that the adjustments parents made to their problems seldom fit the situation of the boy today. Grandfather lived in the country and courted with a horse and buggy, seldom getting ten miles from home. Everyone knew him and his rig, and knew how his courting was progressing. Father went to the county seat to work in a factory. He met a young girl from another city and courted her with a car. His engagement was announced in the home-town paper, but only the family, a few relatives, and his close friends met the girl before the wedding. Son was in the Army. He met, courted, and married a girl halfway across the nation. They flew home for a few days of their honeymoon. His wife worked while he finished college. What will their son do? He will fit the pattern of his generation, and it will be different from the others, continuing the cycle of one generation only partly knowing and understanding the world in which the other lives.

This book has a purpose

Each boy brings with him, at birth, a will to grow, to strive to become himself, to fulfill his destiny. Every boy is born into a family. He will live in this family and be nurtured by it until he steps out as an individual to establish a family of his own. This family will exert some of the most powerful influences on his life. It will develop attitudes toward life that will be with him always. Every boy is also born into a society of his elders with a particular culture which is powerful and persuasive. This society has developed a plan of operation and a set of values to which he must adjust ably and willingly if he is to be happy. Each boy is also born into a society of those of his contemporaries through life, to whom he will look to meet many of his needs. It is the happy triumph of each individual when he can harmonize these forces to build a healthy personality—his inner drives, the cultural expectancies of his family and the community, and the pressures of his own age society, his peer group.

It is hoped that this book will be able to portray clearly and helpfully how these forces can work together for the boy.

CHAPTER 2

What a Boy Needs from His Family

Parenthood is probably the greatest honor ever conferred upon mankind. Being partners in the miracle of creating life elevates a husband and a wife into partnership with the Infinite—who is also Father. If God trusts man to bear and nurture life, man can be assured that he is worthy of that trust and equal to the task. God does not make mistakes.

There are cynics who declare that every occupation requires preparation but parenthood. What would they call life's wondrous plan which provides for the child to be carried within the mother's body, the husband's beloved, for nine months before it is born? Are not their plans, their hopes, their dreams, a preparation? The basic preparation they need is time, so that the love they have for each other can grow to include the life that will be entrusted to them. To fail in this is the only unpardonable error and it does not occur unless the culture in which they live has deprived them of their self-respect and sense of dignity. In this case, the culture must share the blame for their lack of preparation and must give them the understanding and the support they need.

Partnership with the Infinite makes each life of infinite worth. It also sets that life free. A child is not a possession. He is a part of us but belongs not to us. He belongs to himself and life. His life with the family provides the intimate, affectionate, supporting environment which enables him to become a loving being that reaches out toward learning and growth.

The family welcomes a son

Being a boy is pretty sticky living in our land. Patriarchal traditions of Europe continue to exert strong influence on our feelings, despite our contradictory proclamations of sex equality.

The male, in the face of strong scientific evidence to the contrary, is still considered the dominant and stronger sex. He is courage personified, born protector of the weaker sex. He will take the initiative, be the aggressor. He is expected to succeed. As the ultimate sign of male superiority, he alone has the right to carry on the family name. A son is the symbol of family continuity, high success, and national security.

Women often find special joy in bearing a son, not only because of this special social acclaim given him, but also because she may feel that it unites her more closely with her husband in fulfilling his desire for a son and in reproducing a possible likeness of the man she loves.

When "It's a boy!" is announced in the average family, particularly when the first-born, or following a series of sisters, the skirted sex often surrounds him in droves. Dad peers over the women's shoulders, beaming exultantly, and dreaming about baseball games with Son, fishing trips, hikes, camp-outs, and a hundred and one other manly pursuits.

Yes, this differentiation in our attitudes toward the sexes begins at birth. Our culture has developed different ways of loving boys and girls. From the doting of mothers during his infancy, and Dad's rough-and-tumble, hand-on-the-shoulder show of affection, to both parents' tears at high school commencement, sentiment pours over the boy today. He always relies upon it, usually takes advantage of it, yet seldom understands it.

Then there are special ways of smiling at boys, special tones of voice, special ways of playing with them even as infants, and even special colors for their birth announcements, hospital identity bracelets, blankets, clothes. We have our special toys and games for boys as they grow.

Sometimes a generation helps to hold its pride within bounds by joking about its treasures. Everyone knows quips about boys. Boys rarely laugh at these jokes. They're the exclusive property of adults. A speaker can always get a chuckle with "A boy is a noise covered with dust" or "A boy is an appetite with a skin stretched over it."

Adults smile, too, at the picture of a boy with a black eye singing like a cherub in a choir gown. How differently we would feel if it were a little girl wearing the shiner.

To attract attention and to create the inner glow they want us to attach to their product, advertisers portray a boy flexing his muscles, measuring his chest with a tape measure, going fishing. When they put a boy and dog together, the glow is twice as bright.

We tend today to smile at ourselves as we parade these attitudes before our eyes. But there is nothing essentially wrong in setting up such standards of masculinity at various age levels. It is only when we view them as a defense of a sexual superiority, which is becoming increasingly indefensible, that they assume a negative character. In the moral sphere, proceeding from this false assumption, our society—not ideally but actually—still tolerates a masculine permissivity in departure from ethical and religious codes, particularly in the years before marriage.

Slowly we are succeeding in setting up standards of masculinity and femininity that are consistently equal in moral restraints, and equally consistent in exalting the natural superiority of each sex for its own God-given attributes.

We can continue, with these insights, to dream unabashedly our special dreams for our sons (as we dream our special dreams for our daughters). Fortunately these dream boys become real boys and living with them brings parents down to earth. The parent who was sure he would be a better parent than some others he knew experiences many a perplexing and anxious moment. The perfect parent of their dreams experiences many bad days.

There are rewarding days, too, and in these happy moments they see the goal more clearly. They are seeking a youngster who is happy most of the time, who will be friendly and who will be able to contribute to life. They resolve to understand their child. They expect that he will be both like and different from other children and acknowledge that he has that right. They hope they will provide the kind of home which will be secure—a base from which he will be able to move with courage into the world around him. They promise themselves that they will believe in him even when he falls short. He will always be important to them and to the world. Above all, they expect that it will take time to build a personality, and they will rejoice with him as he lives well at each stage of development. These goals are desirable, but just what is the role of the home? What are the responsibilities parents can be expected to carry?

The patriarchal family is disappearing

The role of the home in shaping a boy's life is steadily in transition. It was once the center of much of his economic, social, educational, and religious life. As a boy in a largely agricultural civilization, he was esteemed for his ability to contribute hard labor in felling trees, raising crops, and otherwise helping to sustain his family until he left to establish his own home.

In the old patriarchal home, father was the head of the household, with mother second in authority. In his late teens, her eldest son became a close rival for that secondary position.

While all sons were usually held to rigid obedience to their father, they grew up in a home that provided a living example of the patriarchal authority each boy would assume when he married. Even Scripture was brought forth fortuitously to uphold this alignment of authority. When father spoke, no one else dared utter a word. His was the voice of the judge. He was the source of wisdom.

Rapid industrialization of our society, drawing women—the unmarried, the married and, more recently, the mothers—into office and factory jobs, has delivered women from their full financial dependence upon men. Women have achieved a voice in government—and perhaps an even more emphatic one in the average home today.

In many a modern home, parental authority rests in shared decisions or in an equitable division of authority; also, many families are extending the shared decision-making on many questions to the children, too. These are current and constructive manifestations of the vanishing patriarchal family; they represent the growth of democracy at the place where it should be best learned—in the home, where love and understanding can undergird it strongly.

The boy of today, raised in such an atmosphere, imbibes a new concept, impossible a few short generations ago, concerning his role as a male in society, his role as a future husband.

The picture is not idyllic, of course, since all parents are not following this relatively new, emerging pattern of family organization. In some instances, the wife, often in her rebellion against her patriarchal father, becomes the dominant and nagging partner. Jiggs' wife in the comics, whose husband "escapes" in poker games, and Thurber's Walter Mitty, who "escapes" in dreams, are far from impossible creations. Unpleasant jokes about a neighbor whose wife "wears the pants in the family" reflect both a male longing for a return to patriarchal days and possibly a feminine envy for a woman who has gained ascendancy. The equally rebellious (and equally undemocratic) ultra-feminist intellectual epitomizes this situation, often more subtly though no less penetratingly.

In all these instances, as in the period of patriarchal domination, the unbalanced parental relationship makes its lasting impact upon the growing boy's mind. A wife who nags her husband is likely to become the boy's negative symbol of all womanhood, affecting harmfully all his childhood, adolescent, and adult relationships with the opposite sex. Such a mother can unwittingly lay the foundation for her son's future marriage tensions and possible marital failure. So, too, can a father's attempt to perpetuate a patriarchal family status, for his son will surely marry a girl even freer from the old cultural pattern than his mother is likely to be.

But those who are students of family life believe that the home of today faces its greatest opportunities, that it has more than ever before to offer its children, both spiritually and materially.

Changes in family living

Everyone is aware of many great changes in family life, pronounced since World War I and accelerated since World War II. The family is once again getting larger—but surely not the size of families in our Colonial period of history. Adults have more leisure. The child receives much more attention. The modern middle- and upper-class home is a gem of the mechanical age. There are few significant tasks requiring the child's help. Work tends to be manufactured, to carry on the idea that the child must have home responsibility. Even on the farm, sons are rarely called upon to do the heavy work their own fathers had to do as children. Their work load, little appreciated by urban and suburban boys, has lightened greatly. Mothers in cities and on farms are able more frequently than before to participate in the activities of P.T.A. and other community groups. This is especially evident in families where all the children are in school all day.

There has been great mobility in family life. Families move oftener and move farther. They get farther and farther away from the other members of the family. The greater distance from grandmother, uncles, aunts, and other blood relations reduces the number of persons nearby who care deeply what happens to each other. It may place heavy responsibility upon the few to satisfy the emotional needs of the family members. It also means a breakdown in many of the sex distinctions of home labor. Today, father helps with the dishes and mother helps with the painting. Home is more of a partnership.

Marriage is taking place at a younger age. Divorce is more common. Community attitudes are not as critical of family separation. A high percentage of separations end in remarriage. An increasing number of infants are born outside of wedlock; many are living with only one parent.

Many of the functions formerly carried primarily by the family are now carried by outside agencies and institutions. There has been unprecedented growth in community services in education, recreation, and religious training. This transfer of family functions to outside agencies has caused widespread feeling that the chief objectives of the family have passed away. Some feel that the family is breaking up. Others wonder what place there is for the family.

The greatest changes in the family, however, are not these outer changes. It is easy to see that the heavy oak library table has gone from the parlor, that the steaming wash boiler is no longer on the kitchen stove. No one need regret the passing from the home of this heavy work and drudgery.

Family functions, from much of the preparation of food to the education of the children, have been taken out of the home gradually. Most of these delegations of functions to other agencies have resulted in greater efficiency. They have brought about a renewed awareness of community interdependence that in some localities has approached the spirit inherent in the New England town meeting.

The big changes have been of an inner nature in the greater freedom and honesty between generations, in the shifts of attitudes toward each other and life, and the interdependence of the community.

Along with the great decline in authority, the family is shifting away also from the child-centered home. Current thinking asserts that all persons in the family, adults and youth, are entitled to fulfillment of their personality. It is a family-centered home where strength and support are shared with each other. Today's freedom permits the son to acknowledge that parents are sometimes a problem without feeling guilty about it, and parents can frankly admit that there are moments when they would like to get away from the son forever. No one need feel ungrateful or guilty because family members disagree with each other. There is an acceptance of everyone as a person who has moments of high achievement and moments of failure or mistakes. Families are daring to be lovingly human.

There is greater freedom to express affection between parents, between parents and children, and between children and children. Living together is becoming more satisfying. Families enjoy each other. There is much more emphasis on love and understanding than on authority.

Along with this greater freedom has come a shift away from the mystic toward the real. The female sex is not regarded as an object of awe and admiration, or inferior status, but more as possessing the right to be equal to the male. There is a lessening of the cultural difference between boys and girls and an increase in companionship. The overprotection of girls is disappearing. All of this makes it possible to judge situations more accurately.

Functions of the modern family

Do all of these changes make the family unnecessary? The answer from all studies send back a resounding No. Family life today is more important than ever before. More important problems are faced in the home today than in the homes of a generation ago. Freed from some of the obligations of maintaining prestige for the dominant members and their social and economic roles, today's family life may truly become the place where healthy personalities may grow. What are the major roles of the family? What functions remain within the family circle today? Four very important functions are suggested.

The family is still the place for the reproduction of the race and the meeting of the child's physical needs. The small, intimate group provides the ideal setting where the physical needs of the newborn child can be personally served and where responsibility for the protection and nurture of the new life is gratefully accepted. No human society has devised a better setting for the newborn child to receive the care of his physical needs than is offered in the small family group.

Our culture does not look with favor upon the birth of children outside the family, and both parent and child feel the pressure of society's censure when this occurs. It often makes it difficult for the parent to provide for the basic needs.

The family is still the place for satisfying the basic emotional needs of its members. Every child needs to build an image of himself as a person who has worth, who is valued by others. He needs to know that he belongs, that he counts. This affectionate care and emotional support enables the child to have a picture of the world as a friendly place.

The family provides a secure base from which he can meet life. This need for affectionate support is shared by everyone—no matter what his age. In these days of family dispersal, the home carries a larger and larger role in meeting these affectional needs.

Friends and neighbors will not take the abuse that the family will take. They will not tolerate the expression of angry feelings. But in the family, rebellion can be accepted and understood. And no matter how rude or how thoughtless the child is on occasion, when the anger wears off, the child is still loved and admired.

Home is the place where a child can expect this kind of understanding. He knows what living is like, what values guide the members. Home relieves anxiety and helps the members to feel whole again. It is a place for joy as well as understanding.

Adventure, fun, laughter, and the light touch put sparkle in the eyes of its members.

In the light of this role, it is doubtful that the father who has little time at home with his children can afford to use that time for anything other than loving activity in accordance with the development of the child, if he is to be any positive influence at all. How can he use his time meting out the accumulated punishments of the week, and become anything but an ogre in the mind of the child?

The family is the group that introduces the child into the culture in which he lives. The early behavior of the child will be that which he learns from his parents and from the intimate circle of the family. In this setting he will hear the stories, listen to the songs, learn to eat, learn to speak, begin to work and share. He will identify first with his family, absorbing our culture and mores—as his parents reflect them. Throughout his growing years he will struggle with his parents and be helped by them at the same time.

The family is the group that gives the child his initial identification with the community. The family gives the child a name and a status in the community. It will assume responsibility for his welfare and for his conduct. As he grows, this identity and status will enable him to move into larger groups.

It becomes evident, then, that the major, over-all task of the family is to provide the affectionate, loving support needed by the family members if they are to develop healthy personalities, to provide for children and adults alike the personal intimacy, the affection, the assurance of personal worth which all seek and need. This is the foundation from which all growth proceeds. This emotional environment is created by all the members by their behavior, their attitudes, and their actions. This may be more difficult to achieve than some of the meticulous rules of care and nurture advanced a generation ago, but it is the sort of naturalism practiced by grandmother who felt that children were made to love, recognizing that love is the imperative demand of a creative life. This is true for all members of the family, not just the children. It requires that home be the place where each becomes his best self and becomes creative. This can occur only in an atmosphere of understanding love.

With many of the previous family functions now carried by others, perhaps the family can have more time for the kind of understanding and the mutual support that can produce the genuine family.

The family can best exercise its control through this affection, understanding, and mutual support. Through these means, they can truly affirm the worth of the individual and human brotherhood.

CHAPTER 3

What a Boy Needs from the Community

The boy steps into the community

As a boy grows, he moves into the community and rapidly becomes a part of those about him, first those nearby, and then an ever widening circle that finally, as he reaches maturity, includes all of mankind. As these contacts and associations increase, it is hard to tell whether he takes more of his family pattern into the community or more of the community patterns into the family. When they agree, one supplements the other; where they are in disagreement, he tends to develop a pattern of behavior for each group. Thus the family is not the only group carrying responsibility for the growth and development of the boy. As soon as the boy steps outside the family door, he is in the community and this community carries a responsible role. It has been truly said that if a community has problem children, it is because that community is not a good place in which children can live.

Communities have been accepting this responsibility. They have long recognized the value of youth in society and not only have considered youth as entitled to an opportunity to make good, but have accepted the shared responsibility of providing opportunities to insure that they can become valued members of the community. They have recognized the cost involved in maintaining the boy who does not make good, and also the economic loss if he cannot contribute his share to society. They have further recognized that all their achievements will be passed into his hands, and unless he understands and values them, all their legacy will be dissipated when they are gone.

Since boys will be far more influenced by their experiences in a society than by what the society says, and since boys will ultimately value those things which they feel are valued by society, it is fundamental that society demonstrate the worth it places in its children; that the lives of its leaders illustrate what they preach; and that its laws maintain the freedom under which the individual life can have dignity and meaning.

Public and private agencies serve the boy

Boys are served by all the citizens through government-owned playgrounds, parks, swimming pools, and other recreation and social centers. Most of the group activity is conducted on a mixed-sexes basis, though much is also developed separately for boys, particularly in sports. Educational, speech, vocational, and other guidance services are often provided on an individual-consultation basis. Quasi-public groups like the Police Athletic League concentrate a large share of their attention on boys. The growing public school camping movement and "institutional" camps give increasing numbers of boys the benefits of outdoor living.

Privately supported groups like the Y's, Boy Scouts, and C.Y.O. have developed extensive programs of character-building recreation and service activities for boys. The Y.M.C.A. program now extends from the father-son Y-Indian Guides (sons must be in the 6–9 years bracket), Gra-Y for boys of elementary school age, and Jr. Hi-Y for boys of junior high school age to Hi-Y for boys of high school age. The Y-Indian

Guides are home centered in organizational base; Gra-Y, Jr.-Hi-Y, and Hi-Y are school or community centered. All may be organized like the Cub Scouts, Boy Scouts, and Explorer Scouts, where there is no building maintained by the organization. Where such is the case, these groups rely upon many public and private facilities for meeting places, recreational and social facilities. Like the C.Y.O., each may also be entirely church centered in its organizational base and program emphasis. Churches, through their own organizations, lead the boy to healthy growth through sports, to social growth and spiritual growth.

Hundreds of thousands of untrained volunteer leaders, working under professional staff guidance, give unselfishly of their free time to help boys learn to help themselves through the programs of these and hundreds of other private agencies. These volunteer leaders, ordinary citizens like any of your neighbors, are truly unsung heroes and heroines. Professional group workers marvel constantly at the devotion to youth, the patience, the ingenuity, the strong spiritual motivations—and the growth!—which these adult leaders reveal. They are usually the backbone of privately supported groups. In many smaller communities, public agencies will also tap this vast reservoir of service-minded citizens to extend their program beyond the capacities of their budget-limited staffs.

These volunteer leaders are one of the reasons that private agencies tend to be more personal in their services to groups. Contrastingly, public agencies, offering many facilities impossible with private financing, may tend to become impersonal; and they must necessarily operate within a legal framework.

Both types of agencies are vital to the community. Both demonstrate the growing edge of our democracy wherever they expand and extend their services to the yet unreached thousands of children and youth. Both represent an individual and community concern for their young people. Both depend upon the initiative of individual citizens and groups for their establishment, maintenance, and extension. While both may seem

2. *The group should be limited to boys of his own strength and development,* about those of his own age or grade in school. The best companionship for a boy is other boys of his own maturity. Leadership rises best when a boy is with his peers. Club program and experiences can also be geared to the developmental level of the boys, meeting the needs and interests of a larger proportion of the members. Adventures can be progressive. Adventures are one of the great needs of youth, but they should come when the boy is ready for them. If they come too early, he is robbed of their true thrill. If they come too late, he feels they are childish. Boys of rather wide age range may play games on the playground together, but their differences in social and emotional maturity keep them from being good club members together.

3. *The group should remain small in size and continue to belong to the boys.* A group should be large enough to perform as a group, to have group consciousness, and to require adjustments of each member. It should never be so large that the boy cannot emotionally include all the members as important to him and the group, or so large that the leadership and controls of the group must be taken out of the hands of the boys.

Participation is a fundamental need for growth. The group must not only present opportunities for members to contribute but must depend on their responsible participation, or the experience will lack boy power. The following sizes are recommended:

Boys of 1st, 2nd, and 3rd grades	6 to 9 boys
Boys of 4th, 5th, and 6th grades	7 to 12 boys
Boys of 7th, 8th, and 9th grades	10 to 15 boys
Boys of 10th, 11th, and 12th grades	12 to 18 boys

4. *The group should hold most of its meetings in the neighborhood.* The more a boy travels outside his neighborhood, the more likely is the group to be a collection of individuals, and the less likely it is to secure the interest and support of the

parents. For larger meetings or friendly competition with other groups, some trips out of the neighborhood are desirable, but most of the life of the group should center in the neighborhood where the boys live. Their home community is where their character is formed. As boys grow older, their community grows and association with other groups increases, but they will continue to operate with more ease and power when they have the security of a group close to their own neighborhood.

5. *The group should expect parents and other adults to share in the life of the group.* As a boy moves into the gang state, his parents become less and less of an influence in his life. Only as they are permitted to co-operate with the group through such ways as sponsorship, occasionally enriching the club program, providing special resources, or sharing in club activities, can they retain a significant influence in the life of their boy.

The best groups have the support of their parents. It is a group of parents bringing up a group of boys. Each son is surrounded by many friendly adults at the time when understanding with his own parents is at a low ebb.

6. *The group should have a worthy purpose. It should be associated with some national and international organization, if possible.* Good groups need the assistance of trained supervisors, as good schools need professional teachers. Association with an agency makes for stability and continuity. It assures standards in leadership and program. National agencies provide resources in printed materials and activities far greater than any group of parents can create by itself.

7. *The group should have contacts with other similar groups across the community or city.* Groups must attain standing in the youth life of the community, just as any individual boy must attain standing in the eyes of his associates. Any group which fails to attain this standing eventually loses respect in the eyes of the boys. Teaming up with other groups of the same kind creates the power to do significant things which attract

attention, and gives status to each group. This unity develops a movement. It creates a world of contact and operation that continues to expand as a boy's world should.

8. *The group should have the same leader for several years, if possible.* The first year a leader shares with a group is the hardest year for both the leader and the boys. A changing leadership means continuous strain. The leader who lays his life alongside the life of the group gets to know and understand the group. Boys will listen to the counsel and guidance of this leader.

9. *The group should emphasize group achievement.* The purpose of group experience is to help a boy learn to live with others and to contribute to the life of the group. Good group life seeks the growth of the individual and the improvement of society. It is democracy at its finest. Winning as a member of society apart from the welfare of the group is impossible.

10. *The group should encourage spiritual growth.* The group might not emphasize any creed but it should provide those high points of experience which have religious significance. The big issue of our time is learning to live together. What better set of values for living is there than those taught by the Master Teacher nearly two thousand years ago? The program should seek an interpretation of those values in the daily living of the boys.

CHAPTER 4

The Plan of a Boy's Growth

A boy's growth from infancy to maturity is so natural, follows such a universal pattern, that it is often taken for granted. But taking his growth for granted tempts one to view him too often as a small adult, a little man. Taking his growth for granted also obscures the inner springs of his behavior—the motivations for his boy ways which adults must understand if they are to help him more intelligently.

What, then, are the characteristics of his growth?

Growth in any normal boy is according to plan; it is orderly, sequential, rhythmic. It is varied according to each individual boy. One boy will spurt ahead of other boys his age, then drop behind them, then spurt ahead again. So long as a boy follows the *general* pattern of growth, parents needn't worry about any charts or tables that detail monthly *average* changes. They may rest assured that their boy is normal.

Growth in any normal boy is inevitable, propelling him forward. Sometimes he thrusts forward so fast that adjustment is difficult and painful (even average growth at any time is difficult); he may even voice a regret that he's not still a baby.

Growth for any normal boy is vastly more complex than that of the lower animals. A rat or a beaver born today is much the same as one born ages ago. He builds the same kind of house, uses the same means of transportation, defends himself with the same mechanism, has the same limits in his communication.

Not so the boy born today. Though physically the same, he has better care and opportunity to live—though male infant mortality is still slightly greater than female. He is born into a world unlike even his father's at infancy—a world of television, of jet-propelled and rocket ships, of atomic war and atomic power, of newly discovered planets.

The culture into which he is born has increased its store of knowledge in almost geometrical proportion to that of his father at infancy. As today's boy grows he must adjust to this entirely new world and attempt gradually to assimilate the vast achievements of mankind.

Often parents envy the seemingly carefree life of their sons and yearn for their own childhood. But when they do that, they forget the infinitely more complex world that is developing, the hundreds of new stimuli that impinge upon these growing minds, the bewilderment they would suffer if they were suddenly transplanted to childhood in this age. It is then that parents can thank God that their sons are born with their inherent zest, their continual questing spirit, their internal demand to grow.

How can parents observe and measure this growth to guide them in understanding the general pattern their boy will follow? They can observe and measure it in these four major aspects—physical, intellectual, social, and emotional—all overlapping. In doing so, they can refer to data compiled from the averages of thousands of other children of his chronological or calendar age.

If one views each of the four major kinds of growth longitudinally, from infancy to maturity, he will gain a sense of its orderliness and forward sweep far better than when he examines all aspects of growth at any single stage or age of growth. The latter—the cross-sectional view of each period with its characteristics, a boy's feelings about himself and his world, his developmental tasks—will be detailed after our examination of his longitudinal growth pattern.

Growth is on the inside

The dramatic sequence of growth sometimes makes growth seem simple. If people know what kind of growth a child should be having at any particular time, why not see that such growth occurs? That, of course, is the goal; but the method is not so easy, for growth is not something attached to the individual which one can accelerate or retard with a screw driver adjustment. Growth is within a person, not outside, and can be achieved only by that person. No one else can do it for him. The healthy personality is inside and depends upon that person's feeling toward life, his comfortableness, his contentment, his competence, his peacefulness.

The big question, then, is how does one get inside an individual? And the simple answer is that one does not—experiences do. The only way adults who want to help a boy grow up can be of help is to provide the environment and the opportunities through which the individual himself can grow.

It is somewhat like being a "gardener" in personality. The flower gardener can prepare the soil and plant the seed; he can water it, shelter it, protect it from cold, keep the weeds out, and the seed will grow. He can continue this care and the flower will grow to its richest bloom. He is not responsible for either the color or the fragrance—these were locked up in the seed. His gardening skill provided the opportunity for their fulfillment. That is exactly the role of the adult who seeks to help a boy grow up. He can prepare the environment with all the motivation it can use, he can protect the boy, encourage him, open doors for him, and the boy will grow. The responsibility of the adult is to provide opportunities for the boy to fulfill his life. Having done this, the adult must leave the rest to God, as the flower gardener did with the color and the fragrance of the flower.

This, however, still leaves much for adults to do before they have completed their task. They must provide the conditions for growth.

Conditions encouraging growth

A boy does not need encouragement to grow. He wants to grow. He does not want to stay small either in his physical growth or in his ability to handle life. His entire drive is toward growth, real growth. It is little satisfaction to him just to get bigger and older. How fast or how well he grows depends on the feelings of the adults about him and on the feelings within himself. These feelings are far more important than any set of principles about growth. Feeling free to grow and feeling able to grow are the keys to growth.

Boys grow best when they are with adults who are at ease with them and seem to enjoy them most of the time.

Boys grow best when they are permitted to make mistakes which will not harm them unduly, and are permitted to live with adults who themselves do not pretend to be perfect.

Boys grow best when those about them believe in them and express confidence through words and through giving them freedom.

Boys grow best when those about them understand what purpose they are trying to achieve and team with them or support them in their endeavors.

Boys grow best when those who have authority over them permit them to raise questions, to express doubts, to try out their own ideas.

Boys grow best when they understand the limits of freedom within which they can make decisions, and when this freedom is limited to the responsibility they feel able to carry at their stage of development.

Boys grow best when those about them deal with them with firmness and consistency.

Boys grow best when adults about them behave as adults and show what the grown-up way is like.

Boys grow best when those about them help them when they need help to succeed, but let them struggle when they are winning by themselves.

Boys grow best when those about them gear their expectancy of a child's behavior to his capacity for that behavior.

Boys grow best when those about them understand their developmental needs and provide motivation and opportunities for them to accomplish those tasks.

Boys grow best when they feel strong within themselves, when they feel they are just the kind of person wanted by their family and their friends.

Boys grow best in an atmosphere of friendliness and warmth whether it is with adults or other children. Parental love is the most powerful, most constructive force in a boy's growth.

Boys grow best when they meet actual life situations, emotionally charged, and deal with them constructively, with or without help.

Boys grow best when the tasks they face are suited to their ability and their performance expectancy is related to themselves rather than to the performance of others.

Boys grow best when they are interested in what they are doing for its own sake, and they will be interested when it has meaning to them. Children who are forced to perform a task in which there is no interest or understanding are not helped, but actually blocked. Those who attempt it are battling against human nature and will always lose in the end.

The concept of developmental tasks

The set of principles just advanced describes the conditions under which growth can best be encouraged, but it does not indicate where these principles should be applied. This section is directed to the concept of developmental tasks which holds that there are definitely prescribed tasks at each stage of a boy's life which are practically forced upon him by his own inner drives, the culture in which he lives, or those of his own age group (his peers) with which he lives.

It is as though each individual had a sort of curriculum presented to him or problems to solve at each stage of his growth. He seems to be allowed a certain period of time for the solution of these problems and if they are solved, he is free to move on to the next stage of growth. If they are not solved within this time, he is handicapped, for a new series of problems are presented to him. Because these problems or adjustments come in a definite pattern and at about the same stage of development for all boys, they are called developmental tasks.

A boy seems to meet these tasks most easily when others like himself are working at the same task. They are aided by observing others. To fail in the more crucial of these tasks, when others are mastering them, forces them to face new tasks without the prerequisite achievements, for most of these developmental tasks are related to each other from one stage to the next. The difference at each stage is that the central problem seems to be different.

The boy is often aware of many of these goals but would not consider them as tasks to be accomplished. There are others of which he is not aware, for he cannot explain the feelings within himself nor does he always understand the achievements himself which his culture is pressing upon him. That is why adults can be so helpful; they can provide the encouragement and arrange the opportunities which facilitate the accomplishment of these tasks at the most opportune time.

Whether he accomplishes these tasks or not, time will not wait. If they are accomplished, he will move forward, eager to meet life; if they are not accomplished, time will push him to the end of his adolescence in physical growth and, prepared or unprepared, the culture calls him adult. He uses what he has to meet life, but with a backward look at boyhood or adolescence, reluctant to go.

The specific developmental tasks are identified and explained in the age-range cross sections of life in Chapters 11 through 16 of this book. The major fields in which the specifics have been identified are:

1. Developing a self-image a boy can respect
2. Developing a pattern of affection
3. Achieving independence and self-management
4. Relating one's self to his social group
5. Learning one's sex role
6. Accepting one's body
7. Accepting society's demand for competence
8. Finding one's place in work
9. Finding adventure and joy in living
10. Developing a value system

CHAPTER 5

A Boy's Physical Growth

Infancy (birth through age 2)

Infancy is a period of rapid and unequal growth. Growth of the head slows up and growth of the arms is the most rapid. Trunk growth is the next most rapid. The legs and feet come next in line. Height increases twice as fast in the first nine months as in the second.

Infancy and the first years are also periods of rapid growth in weight. A boy will double his weight in the first four to six months and will gain a total of about 11 pounds in the first nine months. Increase in body weight then slows down and he will gain about 5 pounds in the second nine months.

Muscular strength develops rapidly, starting with the upper portions of the body and moving toward the lower extremities. A child will hold its head erect at four months, sit erect at nine months, stand erect at twelve months, walk with skill distinctly human at eighteen months, and run all over the place at two years.

The brain grows rapidly also. There is a one-third increase in its weight in the first nine or ten months. The rapid development of the skull for the first eighteen months is closely associated with the growth of the brain, eyeballs, teeth, and certain large muscles. Spinal cord weight is quadrupled in the first three years.

The first teeth appear at seven or eight months. The temporary molars appear by the latter part of the second year.

The infant's heart is small compared to the arteries and must beat at a rate of approximately 130 to maintain normal pressure of blood. The heart will increase to twelve times birth size to reach adult size, but the aorta is one-third adult size at birth.

Slightly more than half of the 800 ossification centers to be formed in the human body are present at birth. Formation of the new centers and fusion of the older ones proceed at unequal rates until adulthood. The infant's skeleton has a large portion of cartilage and fibrous tissue. There are 270 bones in the body of the newborn child, as against 206 in adults. Bones and cartilaginous tissue form 15 to 20 per cent of the body weight throughout life.

Metabolism is far more rapid in the period of infancy than in adulthood. The child of three years requires 40 per cent of the food required by an adult, though the body is only 20 per cent of the size.

There is small reserve energy at the beginning and the infant is quickly exhausted, but he steadily gains strength and resistance to disease. (For example, measles in the first year is fatal in approximately one in five cases, and in only one in twenty-five cases from the first to the third year.) Rest is very important and the infant is still sleeping 16 to 18 hours a day at six months, and at least 14 hours a day at twelve months.

The infant uses four to five times as much oxygen as the adult per unit of weight. As he matures, the heart and muscle growth will allow the pulse to drop from 130 at one year to 110–120 at twenty-four months, and 96–100 at thirty-six months.

Early childhood (ages 3–4–5)

Early childhood is marked by a rapid growth of the lower body and extremities, but the pace of big-muscle development exceeds the structural. Gain in height, for example, will be decreased to around 5 inches a year, and gain in weight, to 3 to 5 pounds a year according to body type.

At five or six, he will begin to lose his baby teeth, while calcification of permanent teeth is going on steadily.

The heart continues to grow and the pulse rate drops, reaching 92 to 100. The brain and nervous system continue to develop, the brain approaching adult weight at five or six years of age. Resistance to sickness increases. The boy sleeps around 11½ hours, and his afternoon naps may discontinue at about five years, often earlier.

In this active motor period with strong physical demands, especially in lively play, there is a steady gain in big-muscle development and co-ordination. He begins to bring his physical life under control. He eats at specific times and has approved toilet habits—generally achieved later than if he were a girl.

His motor skills have improved to the point where, at about four years, he can button his clothes, wash himself (don't expect immaculate results!), and brush his teeth. At about five years, he can lace and tie his shoes and put his hat and coat on alone.

Middle childhood (ages 6–7–8)

Middle childhood is a period of relatively slow growth and physical development. By six years a boy has more than doubled his birth length and has reached over half his final height. Weight has increased four to six times and is almost one-third of his adult weight. Head girth has reached nine-tenths of final maturity. The heart has increased to four or five times its weight at birth.

The child begins to lose his first temporary teeth and to gain his first permanent ones.

By the age of eight years, his muscle development will be one-fourth of his body weight. The large muscles of legs and arms will be more developed than the small muscles of the hands and fingers.

Although the body is gaining in resistance (measles—fatal in only one in 250 cases), children of six years and under lose more days of school on account of sickness than do children of any other age. Respiratory disorders reach a maximum about the age of six. There is a great liability to infectious diseases of childhood at this time. Following six years of age, the general health improves rapidly and is never better than at eight years.

The child at this stage uses only twice as much oxygen as an adult per unit of weight, as compared with the infant's use of four to five times as much per unit of weight.

He fatigues easily and needs 11 hours of sleep. Pulse has come down to around 90.

Compared with the ten-year-old, the child of this age period is relatively quiet, but he reaches a new high for his life to date. Motor skills pass sensory development and he is continually on the move.

Late childhood (ages 9–10–11)

Late childhood is a period of abounding health and physical vigor. Illness is rare, but accidents increase due to daring. There is increased co-ordination between physical senses and muscular control. It is a period of slight change in body form, but the muscular, digestive, and circulatory systems are preparing for pubescence.

Growth is relatively slow and continues at about the pace of the previous stage. The body will be ready for a period of rapid growth and change at pubescence.

The boy at eleven years weighs approximately eleven times his birth weight; this is slightly over one-half of his adult weight. He will have about four-fifths of his adult height at twelve years. The heart has grown to seven times its birth weight, and the pulse has dropped to 80–90.

This is the period of greatest activity in life. He loves to test his muscles and his skill against others. Running, jumping, pulling, skating, diving, walking fences, are his delight. Complex acts are mastered as part of a game. He likes speed and wants a high-gear-speed bicycle, or anything to help him cover more ground faster.

Despite great immunity to fatigue and disease, the boy in late childhood should have his rest: at nine years, about 11 hours; at ten years, about 10½ hours; at eleven years, about 10½ hours.

Early adolescence (ages 12–13–14)

Early adolescence is a period of marked physical and structural change.

At pubescence there is a short period of rapid growth as the long bones of the leg and arm stretch. The legs stretch out to approximately four-fifths of their adult length and defy pants legs to keep up with them. Total height is 75 to 85 per cent of final growth. Weight is about two-thirds adult weight. Weight and muscle development fail to keep pace and the boy appears awkward—a lad of elbows and knees.

Although the heart likewise fails to keep pace with bone growth, the pulse rate continues to approach the 72 of adults. The chest widens, deepens, lengthens. The lungs and liver increase in volume and weight. The stomach lengthens and becomes less tubular, and the intestines grow in length and circumference.

By about fourteen years of age, there are some 350 bony masses in the body. After puberty, these decrease rapidly in number, although the final quota of 206 bones will not be reached for several years. The body chemistry to support longer bones and new teeth is now ready.

The pineal and thymus glands halt their probable restraint

of gonadal development. The boy's body is driven forward by the hormones now released in large quantity by these endocrine glands, as well as by the thyroid, pituitary, and adrenals, and absorbed through lymph and blood systems to be circulated all over the body.

The interstitial cells and the testin or testosterone hormone, both produced by the gonads or testicles, are decisive in producing the distinctively masculine physical and psychical qualities. The sex organs increase in size. Pubic hair appears, along with a considerable hair growth in the armpits; the beard comes into evidence, with the hair longer, coarser, more pigmented (he may ask Dad for a loan of his razor—proudly). A boy's larynx enlarges, making his "Adam's apple" more prominent, and vocal cords lengthen, producing his "change of voice." His face loses its fatty tissue and the flesh feels harder; facial contours become more angular, with a heavier and stronger lower jaw. As his reproductive functions develop, the boy usually experiences his first nocturnal emissions. This may occur early or late in adolescence and should be considered perfectly normal. It is important for a boy to be prepared in advance for this experience, to avoid any fear of abnormality or "loss of manhood" with each emission.

Health is usually excellent in early adolescence, and there is a strong resistance to disease. Appetite is tremendous (as Mother's food bills will testify) and favorite foods are often taken to excess. Acne often troubles boys at this time.

There are seasons when the boy has a sense of power and accuracy of movement, and seasons when he seems weak, clumsy, and unco-ordinated. Team games and organizations are now the boy's strong favorites, and there is a decrease in running and romping on his own. There is a strong tendency to overdo in sports. Because his nervous system is still unstable, he still needs ample rest: at twelve years, about 10 hours; at thirteen, about 9¾ hours; at fourteen, about 9¼ hours.

Middle adolescence (ages 15–16–17)

In middle adolescence the body now begins to round out toward adult proportions. The muscle fiber becomes thicker and longer and begins to catch up with the rapid bone growth of the previous period. The circumference of the face, arm, upper arm, calf, and thigh increases. At sixteen years, the muscles are about 44.2 per cent of the body weight. Strength increases, and at sixteen years of age is roughly double the strength at eleven years.

Ratio of heart muscle to length of body increases twice as fast as before adolescence. At the end of this period the heart is ten to twelve times birth weight. Blood vessels grow in length and area of cross section. Walls become thicker and stronger. Lungs increase in size, capacity, and power. The rate of breathing is slower but volume of air inhaled and exhaled is increased greatly. Tremendous energy and vigor from the strong flow of blood (increased blood pressure), increased oxygen, and general body conditions make for excellent health, excellent resistance to disease, and excellent recuperative power.

There is a continued resistance to fatigue and a slight decrease in sleep needs. All ages of this period need about 9 hours of sleep.

The daily food needs reach a maximum at sixteen years. Dietitians suggest generous amounts of milk; cocoa; whole-wheat bread; toast; cereals; salads made from fresh fruits or green vegetables; meat substitutes containing eggs or cheese; moderate lean meats; puddings containing milk, bread, or cornstarch; nuts; raisins; plain cakes and cookies; fruit, milk, and eggs; pies with little crust; warm biscuits, muffins, water at and between meals.

Return of muscle proportions harmonious with over-all body proportions makes for body balance, poise, and grace.

Late adolescence (ages 18–19–20)

Growth is greatly retarded as the body continues to increase in height, weight, and strength, approaching manhood. Chest girth continues to expand until it exceeds one-half the person's height. The body is knitting itself together in preparation for the demands of maturity. There is a gradual increase in bone cross section and in uniting of ossification centers.

All these mean increased power, skill, and capacity for endurance. The body functions as that of an adult, but strength and capacity for endurance are still increasing. Motor ability continues to improve, especially in periods of training, and the body is approaching peak performance in balance, poise, and grace. Regular hours, wholesome food, vigorous activity, and 8 hours of sleep will aid this increased growth.

Manhood

The body is mature structurally when it has had the opportunity and the time to reach adult proportions. It must be able to stand the strain placed upon it by normal daily living and to withstand reasonable shock caused by sudden change.

Maintenance of this mature performance demands care on the part of the adult in regard to all reasonable matters of health, such as regular physical examinations, proper diet, adequate rest, vigorous activity, and observance of the other well-known health habits.

The body is mature functionally when it is able to maintain the vitality, health, and endurance of an adult body. It must be able to resist disease and respond quickly to the will of the person, actively and sympathetically, at peak performance. There must be muscular strength to maintain good posture at rest or in motion. There must be well-developed heart and lungs to support the body at work and in play without undue fatigue. There must be rhythm, balance, and grace in the perfectly mature body.

Maintenance of this mature performance demands that the person keep a healthy outlook on life and have proper attitudes toward the body and the service he expects it to give to him. He must be able to satisfy the body demands for continuous efficient functioning.

CHAPTER 6

A Boy's Mental Growth

Infancy (birth through age 2)

The early years of life are primarily a period of sensory development. The infant reacts very early to gross stimuli, such as darkness, light, pain, and loud sounds. He can differentiate tones from his mother very early, for these are accompanied by physical sensations.

In learning to talk, he will pass through what is called the babbling stage, or play with sounds, and the naming stage to the question stage, in the first three years. At three months he will coo when contented and whimper when uncomfortable; at nine months he may say "da-da" or "ma-ma"; at twelve months he will understand simple commands and may say four words, though the average boy, many experts believe, is slightly slower than his sister in vocabulary growth. After eighteen months, the pace quickens and simple sentences soon come into use.

There is rapid growth in perception. Sound, color, size, weight, and shape will be differentiated during this period. There is rapid development in ear-eye associations and the eye-hand and ear-hand co-ordination.

Curiosity is ever present and is very actively expressed through questions at the end of the period. His natural, innocent, and harmless exploration leads him at about one year to discover his genitals, just as he discovers fingers, toes, ears, and nose. Every new object is usually put in his mouth, and finger-sucking may continue.

Play becomes imaginative by the end of the period, and the infant will develop many ways of entertaining himself.

Early childhood (ages 3–4–5)

Curiosity continues to increase and questions are constantly on his tongue. There are many records of over three hundred questions a day by the three-year-old child.

His senses become sharper, especially his sense of distance and time. Interest in color and shape increases. There will be increased appreciation of music.

Imagination develops and he lives in a dramatic world. Fairy tales are a source of great enjoyment. Imaginary companions are common. His imagination will lead to falsehoods as he builds his own stories. This is the time to tell him good stories.

The child is very active without much purpose. Ears and eyes take in everything. He takes everything he can reach and tries to use it in some way.

Language continues to improve. He learns and remembers many things about him. Rhymes and stories are learned rapidly. He enjoys repetition and likes stories read and reread.

His ability to carry out directions increases rapidly. By the end of the period he can perform errands with three or four separate instructions.

Middle childhood (ages 6–7–8)

Questioning started earlier but middle childhood is the beginning of more probing questions. Questions are no longer the "why" type, they deal with "how" and "what."

Imagination continues to develop, becoming more day-dreaming as interest in fairy tales fades and interest in heroes increases. His individualism is very strong, and he sees himself as a jet pilot, baseball or cowboy hero, a Robin Hood or Captain Kidd. He increases his experimentation with everything, and this is the period of "dirt, noise, questions, measles, bumps, mumps, and broken bones." He prefers Western or adventure plots in radio, movie, or TV programs, and his games take on these characteristics as fear lessens and courage develops through the dares of his playmates. His pockets become miniature museums, for he collects everything. He loves a good time.

These are days when he is introduced to the first grade, and usually begins there to learn the tools of the culture—reading, writing, and numbers. At first these may be labored, but joy increases as his sense of achievement advances. It is no longer considered a cause for alarm if a child does not read early in life. It is important that he have the right kind of help when the reading readiness appears; this reading readiness includes not only a desire to learn to read, but proper ocular muscle development, as well.

Late childhood (ages 9–10–11)

Late childhood is a period of rapid mental growth. This is often considered the school period when the boy makes great progress in reading, writing, and arithmetic, and lays a foundation for general education. Interest in rhymes and riddles is high and he often attempts rhymes and stories of his own.

The boy is experimenting with everything—the spirit of adventure is high. The sense organs are still improving, with discrimination and observation especially keen.

Concentrating ability has increased and the boy does more reading. Adventure and biography are his first choices. He has an interest in the use of his hands and is more patient and skillful in crafts. Boys begin to ignore girls as the differences in their interests increase. Exploration is at its height and boys are continually getting into difficulties and getting out again. Confidence and courage increase as they are successful. Adults get anxious and want to solve their problems for them, to keep them out of trouble. Boys resent it and it is good that they do.

Early adolescence (ages 12–13–14)

In early adolescence the boy is approaching adults in test intelligence. This is the big day of leadership and it demands skill in getting along with those of his own age and sex. A will of his own develops as he goes out with his own kind. He loves excitement and adventure. Adventure movies are his first choice, with historical, sport, comedy, and mystery pictures following in that order. The imagination becomes creative. New interests appeal. He imitates adults who are favorites. Skills improve.

He does abstract thinking, examines evidence critically, loves to argue. He needs opportunity to make many of his own decisions. Memory is excellent. He has increased ability to adjust to obstacles. He can look ahead and plan a course of action to achieve a goal. Along with this increase of reasoning comes a decrease in making things unless they have a definite purpose.

Toward the end of this period his reading of magazines increases. There is a waning interest in adventure stories and increased interest in athletics, invention, technical mechanics, history, and travel. Interest in the larger world of vocations is beginning.

Middle adolescence (ages 15–16–17)

The middle adolescent has increased ability to think for himself, to make decisions, to carry out plans of his own making, to do things for a purpose. He has increased ability to use his past experience in making his judgments. He loves to argue mostly for the sake of argument or to resist the adult world. Part of the arguments come from the doubts and questions that concern him about right, wrong, church, God, girls, friends, popularity, and all the things that have risen to challenge his feeling that he is a man. He becomes concerned about lifework or college and may make concrete plans for his future. He has a strong sense of justice and fair play.

Skills improve rapidly if given free play—but success with friends and adjustments with members of the opposite sex may take time from lessons and skills.

Reading is little different from adult reading. Interests are more individual and specialized. Reason, memory, judgment, and attention develop fairly regularly from childhood through the teens. Responsibilities which include his co-operation, judgment, and initiation have greater interest.

Late adolescence (ages 18–19–20)

The late adolescent begins to see himself in relation to his growing world of people and problems. He begins to see more clearly the demands of adult life. He thinks of himself in relation to these and perhaps to the home of which he may picture himself as the head. As his sense of responsibility develops, he strives to sharpen his mind and improve his skills to achieve the success he pictures.

The conflicts between himself and the world are very real.

Manhood

The mature person mentally is one who is willing to be a part of life, who meets life squarely, head up, and who develops increasing ability to solve problems as they arise in ways that are most satisfying over the longest period of time.

He has ability to look ahead, to plan a course of activity to achieve a desired goal, and to push that goal ever farther and farther as he achieves it step by step.

The mentally mature person comprehends the plan of the universe and the part he must play to meet the demands of that life.

CHAPTER 7

A Boy's Social Growth

Infancy (birth through age 2)

The mother (or the person caring for his physical needs) is the infant's first society. Brothers, sisters, and father gradually become a part of this society as they present themselves to him in his daily living. These persons nearest him who care for his physical needs make the world which gives him his first social response.

The infant's first role in his social world is rather autocratic, demanding immediate satisfaction and physical comfort. These demands come from simple animal functions of the body, and pleasure or comfort is experienced as these are satisfied.

As the baby grows older, he meets more and more people and finds that his desires often conflict with theirs, that his supposed rights may not be accepted by others, that all property is not his, that some things are considered bad and must not be done.

During the first two years, the child lives pretty much by himself except in relation to those who are always about him. He will play in company with another child, but not with him.

His autocratic role breaks down as people cease to jump at

every beck and call to give immediate satisfaction, and he moves into a highly self-asserting individualism.

Some of his social achievements have been listed as follows:

6 months	Conscious of strangers
9 months	May know trick like peek-a-boo
12 months	Co-operates while being dressed
18 months	Bowel control practically established
	Uses spoon without much spilling
2 years	Bladder control established
	Listens to stories with pictures
	Asks for things at table by name
3 years	Can open door
	Put away his toys
	Cross street alone

Early childhood (ages 3–4–5)

Early childhood is a period of individualism which will last for some time. It is most marked in the preschool period where the child's experience with others of his own age is apt to be more limited. Other children of his own age will do most to aid his development through this stage eventually, but right now the child seeks the approval of his family circle, especially his mother and other adults intimately associated with her.

He begins to seek playmates but play is more parallel play than with the group. In his first contacts with the group, he uses the "grab" method of getting the desired object that the other child is using. Adult guidance is needed on sharing what can be shared.

He finds he is continually running into difficulties and does not understand why. Most of the answers given to his questions of "why" are meaningless. He has no principles upon which to work and it is mostly a trial-and-error period of finding that some things are considered good, some things are considered bad, some things can be done, some things must be avoided.

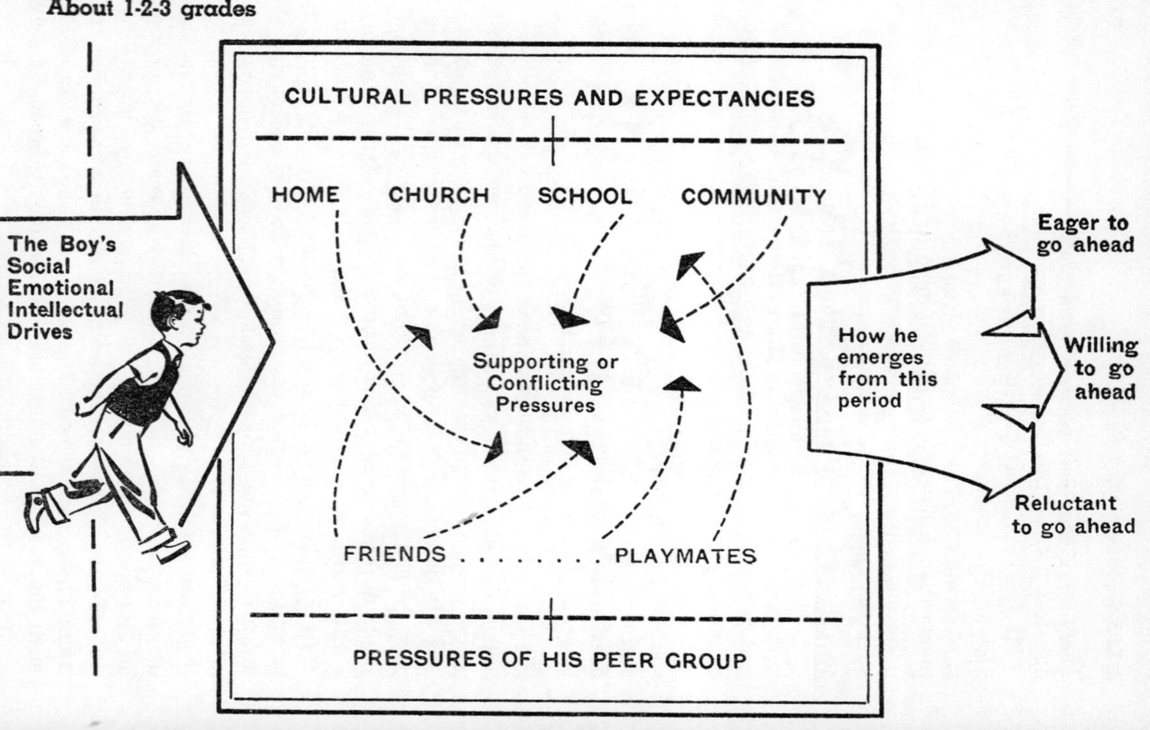
Ages 6-7-8 years
About 1-2-3 grades
The Boy's
Social
Emotional
Intellectual
Drives
CULTURAL PRESSURES AND EXPECTANCIES
HOME
CHURCH
SCHOOL
COMMUNITY
Supporting or
Conflicting
Pressures
FRIENDS . . . . PLAYMATES
PRESSURES OF HIS PEER GROUP
How he
emerges
from this
period
Eager to
go ahead
Willing
to go
ahead
Reluctant
to go ahead

There are even some things that cannot be said or about which one does not ask questions.

He sees people get mad at things which he does. Even punishment is introduced. Yet he finds it a happy world, though most bewildering, and he wants to be a part of it. He wants to please the adults because they seem to be the most powerful.

He finds little room for self-expression. Nobody pays much attention to his wishes, while he has to obey everybody.

Middle childhood (ages 6–7–8)

In middle childhood a boy has greater ability to move about and to handle himself in the physical world. He does not need so much adult attention and he meets more people of his own age, people who are like himself. This is especially true as he starts to school. In addition to meeting other children, he meets an increasing number of other adults who place demands upon him. More and more he finds that he must do certain things to grow up and be accepted in society. He imitates others who get the most approval, not to be like them as much as to have his individualized self get similar or more approval.

He is no longer dependent upon the family circle for social response. He gets out and plays with children, and finds more and more ways to work and play with people. He shows greater ability to co-operate in his play and spends hours with other children in dramatic play, imitating the activities of fathers, mothers, and persons with whom they are familiar.

He finds himself more and more able to meet his equals. If he insists on having his own way, he may have to fight for it. Again he finds himself involved in social ideas, without reasons or explanations. If he fights another boy, not much is said, but if he hits a girl he gets punished. If he fights with his fists, he may lose, but if he resorts to sticks or stones to aid him, he gets into trouble.

Gradually he discovers the reasons for rules in a game and triumphantly calls them to his aid. He is forced to accept them when the rules are against himself. He finally begins to help

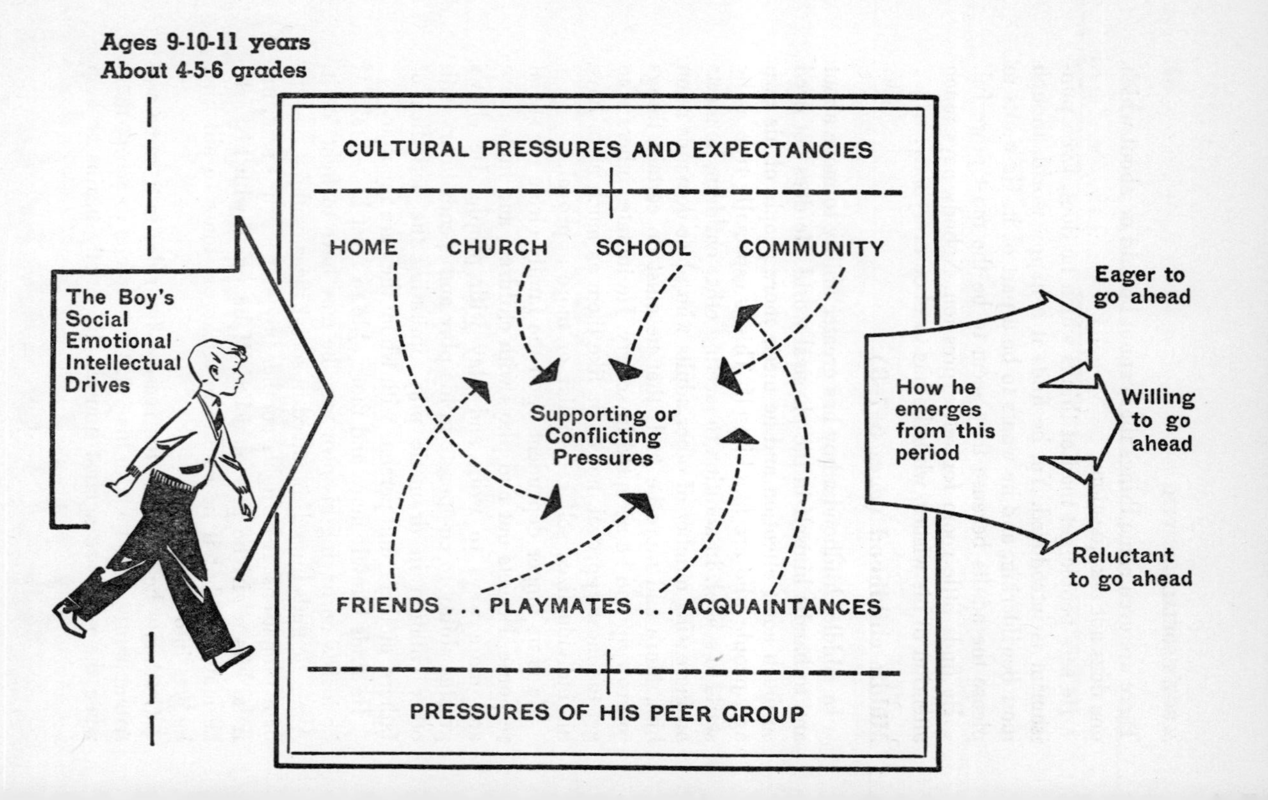
Ages 9-10-11 years
About 4-5-6 grades
The Boy's
Social
Emotional
Intellectual
Drives
CULTURAL PRESSURES AND EXPECTANCIES
HOME
CHURCH
SCHOOL
COMMUNITY
Supporting or
Conflicting
Pressures
FRIENDS . . . PLAYMATES . . . ACQUAINTANCES
PRESSURES OF HIS PEER GROUP
How he
emerges
from this
period
Eager to
go ahead
Willing
to go
ahead
Reluctant
to go ahead

make and enforce rules with the others. He likes games of low organization which stress individual competition. Tag games are the favorite sport of this period. He finds more pleasure in playing with others. He begins to come into a co-operative period of work and play, and the influence of the playmate of his own age is apparent.

Late childhood (ages 9–10–11)

Much as he likes to assert himself, the boy in late childhood has discovered that he has better times if he co-operates. He also begins to want the approval of these playmates, even more than the approval of his parents. He begins to form gangs, clubs, with his playmates. These clubs have codes, passwords, and prized secrets. The boys who are strong and skillful in games will be the leaders. Each member must solve his own fights and troubles within the group, but the group will stand together against outsiders. Loyalties develop and the boy strives for leadership among his kind. (The wise parent takes advantage of some proven organization, such as the Y.M.C.A., Boy Scouts, or C.Y.O., for supervision and development of the better values of this club interest, for without supervision it has touches that are often selfish, savage, and even cruel.)

This is the time the boy plays the most games, takes the most dares, has plenty of fights, and is busy all of the time. He hangs his clothes on the floor, comes to the table dirty, forgets what has been told him about manners, believes girls are worthless, and begins to think Dad isn't as wise as he used to view him. He is curious about everything, talks modern inventions with other boys, and knows more about cars and airplanes than most parents.

He continues to find that society demands certain things before he is accepted. He finds conflicts between the club, society, and himself. He can't see his way out but learns to control his emotions because of group demands, and he tries to work

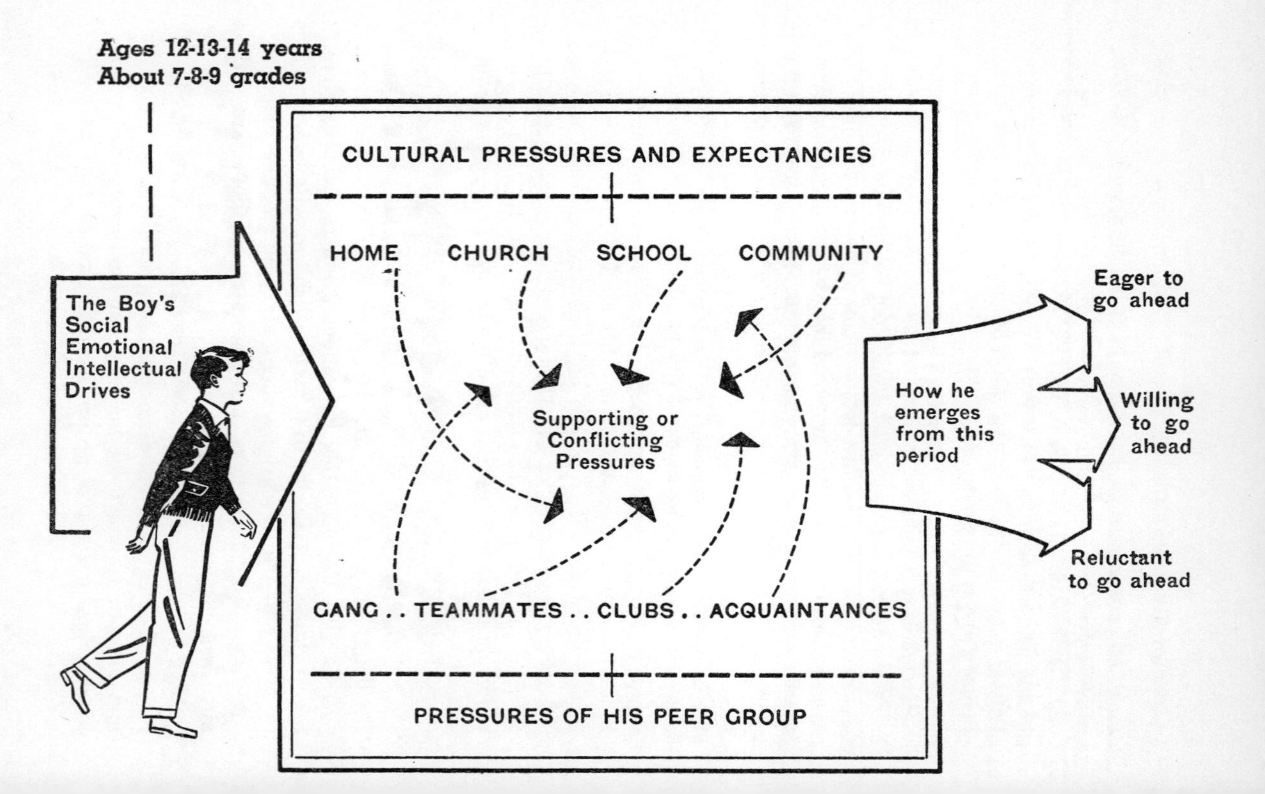
Ages 12-13-14 years
About 7-8-9 grades
The Boy's
Social
Emotional
Intellectual
Drives
CULTURAL PRESSURES AND EXPECTANCIES
HOME CHURCH SCHOOL COMMUNITY
Supporting or
Conflicting
Pressures
GANG . . TEAMMATES . . CLUBS . . ACQUAINTANCES
PRESSURES OF HIS PEER GROUP
How he
emerges
from this
period
Eager to
go ahead
Willing
to go
ahead
Reluctant
to go ahead

out a compromise set of habits to meet all situations. When emotions are uncontrolled, it will usually be at home.

The individual play tends to be rough and noisy at the beginning of this period, but team play gradually replaces individual play. Games and sports become more complex, and competitive games with other groups begin to claim his attention.

Parents may find it difficult to adjust to this stage, for the boy places the gang approval and activities ahead of that of the parents. But if they understand that this is one of the normal, desirable stages in growing up socially, they can cooperate with the boy the same as in other stages. He does not want parents to try to be his age or be his chum. He wants children of his own age for associates and he needs his parents as comforters and confidants who will give guidance in an understanding way at times when he is ready and eager for it.

Early adolescence (ages 12–13–14)

Early adolescence is the heyday of loyalty to those of a boy's own age and sex. Parents are more and more out of the picture as the boy responds to the demands of the group. He sees himself through the eyes of his associates and craves their approval of his acts and his appearance. He will even go so far as to cite his friends as his authority over wiser proven facts. The group often takes on more club organization and the boys assume increasing responsibility for their own direction.

The physical change in body marks the preparation for the next stage in social maturation. A boy becomes self-conscious, largely through the comments and teasing of other people at his voice changing, his growing, or his new attraction for the opposite sex. The girls that were, for a period, considered worthless now begin to take an honored place in his attention. This interest may express itself in teasing, tripping, or actual dating, but seldom will one boy and one girl spend much time together alone. Usually it will be several boys and several

Ages 15-16-17 years
About 10-11-12 grades

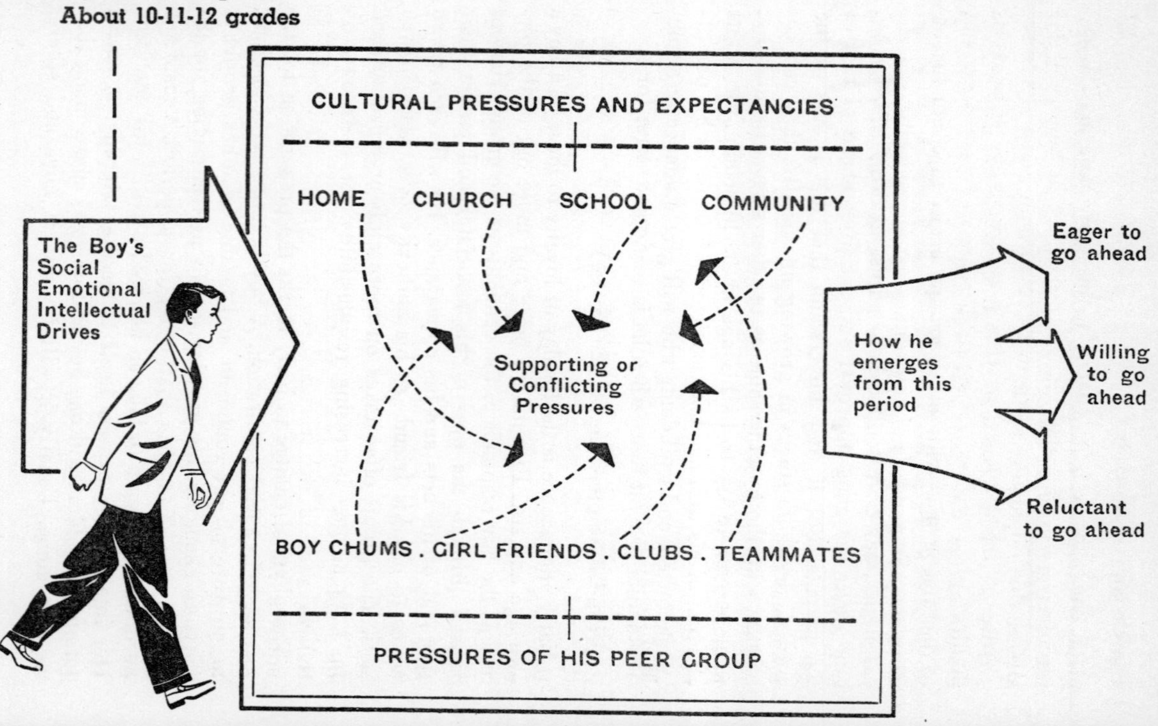

girls, several boys and one girl, a sandwich date, double dating or larger groups. The boy is afraid of those long spells of silence that might occur if he were alone with a girl.

This period is accompanied by some confusion. Since girls mature earlier than boys, they are impatient with the antics of the boys of their own age, and often go out with older boys. Boys do not understand this difference in maturity and the resulting rivalry and jealousy add to their difficulty in this new adjustment. Another problem for the boy is that he now has periods when he feels like a man, but the family still looks upon him as a boy.

The conflicts of this period tend to ease as he makes his adjustments for the next stage where boy chums and girl friends are the normal development.

Middle adolescence (ages 15–16–17)

Although the middle adolescent continues as a member of the group or club and gets many of his basic satisfactions in the club, he begins to be drawn more toward certain boys who are most like himself, as he forms special friends and chums. These are the boys who share his inner hopes, ideals, and ambitions as he views himself as a man. A strong sense of justice and fairness is exhibited and he appreciates square dealing. He is very much aware of himself as a person and wants to go it alone. He has experienced the demands of society upon his conduct and now makes standards of his own, based upon the demands of his friends, those he respects and those he admires. He bases these standards on a high level, with some concessions to the adult world that he longs to enter and where he wants to be accepted.

He seeks social success with both sexes. His social experience and success with boys has been gradually achieved, but he is inexperienced in how to win this success with the girls. His sense of self is very high; he asserts himself strongly to be noticed and will overassert himself if he is not recognized on socially approved levels. He is most concerned about his physical appearance and this is the period of highest clothes consciousness.

Team games and organization are still the favorite sport, though an increasing number sit in the stands and cheer for outstanding performers, and share in their successes as friends, members of a club, or students in the school. Many have moved toward small group sports with friends, such as tennis, golf, driving a car, operating a boat, or using a gun.

Late adolescence (ages 18–19–20)

For the late adolescent, an important achievement following close friendship with a few chums of his own sex is the achievement of successful social status with the other sex, upon a level where he enjoys giving of himself (even at some sacrifice) in order that those most attractive to him will be happy. Out of these associations with the other sex he selects the ones most suited to him, to whom he gives love and from whom he is capable of winning love.

Along with this experience of love giving comes a greater tolerance for others and a growing recognition of the sacredness of personality.

The young man becomes conscious of membership in more and larger groups of society.

Manhood

The person who is socially mature enjoys the company of other people. He finds it possible to enter into their groups through sincere interest in their undertakings and their interests. His tolerance has broadened to include others outside his own intimate circle and he willingly sacrifices in social causes with them for the greater social good.

The normal course is for the man to select some one person of the other sex whom he loves and to establish his family and home with her, where their baby son will start this socializing cycle anew.

CHAPTER 8

A Boy's Emotional Growth

Infancy (birth through age 2)

The new member of the family soon learns that people respond in different ways to his different expressions and he experiences pleasure or dissatisfaction in the type of response given to his demands. He also notices different voice tones and he learns to expect different handling with different tones. In addition to pleasure attending the care of his physical needs, he learns to depend upon the cuddling, fondling, and love of this first social world.

Through these first loving contacts he comes to feel that the world is a friendly place, that he can trust it, that things have a way of continuing to exist. He needs these feelings of confidence if he is to take his next step in emotional growth.

Love is essential for all human beings. They need it as much as they need food and sunshine if they are to grow. The infant's first love comes from his mother. He depends upon this love and it is revealed to him daily in the physical care he receives, and the coddling he experiences. During this period the infant is wholly centered in himself and seeks his own satisfaction and comfort. His response to any discomfort is an insistent demand for attention, and he takes the attention he receives for granted. He expects the same attention and care from others that are about him. As he gets to know those about him, he learns how to win them to do what he wants for his own satisfaction and he resists any direct attempt to change his idea.

In these early years, as his body grows and he starts moving about, he begins to discover himself as an individual. He begins to test his environment and those around him. He begins to become difficult to live with and his defiant No often bothers adults. These are all a part of trying to assert himself as an individual who wants to belong and be considered of worth.

Early childhood (ages 3–4–5)

The period of early childhood is marked by a shift to include the love of his parents with a love of himself. While still very much wrapped up in himself, he occasionally shows that he likes to please the adults who are nearest him (probably his parents).

This is not as important to him, however, as getting acquainted with the interesting world about him and trying things out. He needs to be encouraged to help himself and to be well supplied with opportunities to try his creative ideas. Celebrating his efforts is as important as appreciating his results, for he needs to feel within himself that he is able to do these things. Conscience is developing and he needs to adjust his behavior to it, with a happy outcome.

Middle childhood (ages 6–7–8)

Middle childhood is another period when he seeks parents' approval and he discovers that his pleasure doesn't need to be at the expense of the sacrifice of others. In fact he finds that he feels better when others are happy. By the end of this stage, he will enjoy seeing pleasure on the faces of those with whom he plays because it makes him feel happy, too.

As he contacts brothers, sisters, and others about his own age, he finds them wrapped up in themselves as much as he is wrapped up within himself. All of them are interested in themselves. They are willing to please adults because they are often receiving love from them, but those of his own age are as selfish as he is; and he has no desire to please them because they will give nothing in return. He can exploit his parents, but not children of his own age.

The results of this selfishness are seen in the confusion and many fights of the playground. Gradually the child discovers that he gets his own way more by considering the wishes of others. Only when everyone is willing to co-operate can the games be a success and fun. As these group contacts are multiplied and the child has opportunity to participate in co-operative games, he increases his skill in this and in other ways. He needs to feel that he is good at something. This is especially important to him. At this age he likes to play, but finds it especially hard to lose. His ego is not yet able to take many of these blows.

Late childhood (ages 9–10–11)

Late childhood is the stage where co-operation is demanded, for a boy is beginning to shift his anchors of security from the home toward the gang or toward groups of his own age and sex. Basic to acceptance by any group is a feeling that one has ability or accomplishments that can contribute to the group. In addition, the group demands co-operation as one of the prices of membership, and frowns on selfish demands or lack of emotional control. The fear of being a sissy is worse than fear of danger, and a boy may take risks and even defy adults, to prove his readiness for activities with the group and win their approval. Co-operative ability is one of the things learned with the group that he will need to improve and enlarge throughout life. This period is a great practice time in law abiding, conforming, and fitting in with others.

Parents may be alarmed at the authority the boy bestows

upon the group of his own age and sex. They should acknowledge it as one of the signs that their boy is growing up. He still loves his home and depends upon it, but does not want that love to be expressed toward him by coddling or expressions such as were used when he was an infant. He feels that he can do more things for himself. It is tremendously important for the parent to take a helpful interest in the activities of the group. This does not mean imposing of the parent's will, but rather implies helping the boys do the things they want to do at a level where they can participate and experience satisfactory achievement.

This is the last stage in preparation for a complete shift from the home to the world of his peers as seen in the club. He should have learned to endure some pain or discomfort and meet some difficulties without acting like a baby; he should be willing to work toward some goal at the cost of some sacrifice and he should be able to work with others of his own age toward a goal that has meaning to them as well as to himself.

Early adolescence (ages 12–13–14)

Early adolescence is the stage where craving for companionship with others like himself is the strongest. He will be uncomfortable and unhappy outside of the group. Any fear that the group would not want or accept him will affect his personality. He needs to feel accepted and sought. He has pulled his security anchor from the home and placed it with the group. The group approval takes the place of the approval earlier sought from the parents.

The outstanding characteristics of this stage are the successful adjustment to those of his own age and sex and the beginnings of romantic interest in the other sex. He still depends on the love of his parents, but feels himself more adult and able to do most things for himself. His social intelligence and success should be aiding him in developing poise and ability to meet ordinary situations without emotional display.

Middle adolescence (ages 15–16–17)

Middle adolescence is the stage of intimate friendship with selected members of his own sex, and of romantic love with those of the opposite sex who are approved by his peers. He not only seeks continued popularity but also wants to win and give love. These are the days of his first big love affairs (whether puppy love, crushes, love-at-first-sight, or the real thing). This romantic love cannot develop unless a boy has passed the stage of love of himself and learned to be happy when others are happy. A boy may appear to have a romance because of interest in the other sex, but if it is based on the enhancement of his own ego and not a desire to make the other person happy, it is still an infantile love.

The adolescent is very much aware of his feelings of being a man. His feelings of adequacy and self-assurance come from his proven skills, living interests, and his past successful achievements. All these make him feel able to play a significant masculine role in the world.

He finds conflicts between his desire to be on his own, the desire for independence and for adventure, and the desire to be accepted in the adult world. Parents will need to be patient and aid his need for faith in himself in spite of the fact that he probably considers his home life humdrum and monotonous, and his parents decidedly behind the times. Wise parents will encourage his growth and recognize the tremendous development this romantic interest will mean to their son. They will not tease or laugh about it and will certainly be cautious about prying into it. He will choose the kind of girls his earlier experiences have demanded of him. There is little the parents can do about it now.

Late adolescence (ages 18–19–20)

As romantic love develops, the youth in late adolescence pictures himself more and more as a man of the world, as the head of a family of his own. He has arrived at a place where he is able to go beyond himself and finds himself at one with others. He seeks more and more freedom from the family, but will have a growing appreciation of his home, especially if he goes away.

Mistakes and misunderstandings are still upsetting. He longs for new experience, for opportunity at adult tasks. His scheme of values takes sharper form and he finds pleasure in achieving for himself. But he also goes farther and finds pleasure in helping the people he loves to achieve goals they need, too.

Manhood

The emotionally mature person is one who faces life squarely and makes intelligent changes to meet the situation rather than being blindly persistent in his previous position and fighting stubbornly to maintain it. He sees the situation as it really is, and he is free from emotional conflicts and unreasonable fears or anxieties as he goes to meet it. He knows and expects that change will come, and he tries to adjust himself in the best interests of himself and his fellows. These adjustments are approached with the confidence and poise of having succeeded in previous situations.

The emotionally mature person feels a responsibility to give of himself without seeking in return. He feels and is able to express anger at injustice and is capable of deep sympathy for those in difficulty. He is able to contribute to the well-being of those about him rather than demanding of them to satisfy his own social need.

The emotionally mature person has achieved an emancipation from his parents, but has an understanding respect and friendship for them and an appreciation of what they tried to do for him.

The emotionally mature person has capacity for the love of a mate and is capable of giving as intensely here, without expecting anything in return, as in any other relationship. This is especially true in relation to his own children, where his own son will live this cycle anew.

Some thoughts on maturity

The description of maturity at the close of each sequence of growth tends to give the impression that maturity is some fixed state of perfection. Nothing could be farther from the truth. Maturity is not some fixed point where a person has suddenly become adult and remains there, forever mature. In one sense a boy may be mature at each stage of development, for boyhood is rich and meaningful in itself.

In its greatest sense, maturity is an ever advancing goal toward which one moves through all the days that are his. The only fixed point is the line where one passes from infancy to adulthood. That line is where one begins to contribute more to life than he takes from it.

CHAPTER 9

Why a Boy Behaves as He Does

It is not a slam at you when people are rude—
It's a slam at the people they have met before.
F. SCOTT FITZGERALD, *The Last Tycoon*

"How do boys get the way they are?" "Why on earth did he do it?" "Haven't I told you a dozen times?" "Wasn't he wonderful?" "If he would always be like that. I was so proud of him!" These are the questions and the comments one hears whenever behavior is under discussion.

Boys are not born the way they are. That is certain. They are not born with manners or as basketball players. These are acquired skills. They are not born Methodists or Republicans. These are cultural inheritances. They are born with inner personal drives and they are born into a culture. What they become and how they behave is the culmination of their experience with these two forces.

What is behavior?

Behavior is the detail of living within the growth sequence. It is the response of the individual to his environment at any given moment. Each person brings to life certain drives within him. He brings a will to grow and an eagerness for competence. He also brings a high sense of self. From the very beginning this self is in competition with its environment. If the self finds its environment friendly and loving, the will to grow asserts itself and the boy is eager to grow. If, however, the self finds the environment unfriendly and feels that it has to defend itself, it will expend its energy defending itself and will not be able to grow. The foundation upon which growth and learning depend is love. This is true throughout life, for no person can be free to grow in love and understanding toward others when he is forced to defend himself. Those who cannot learn to consider others necessarily must remain infantile.

It is important to remember that children act first in accordance with these inner drives and feelings about the self. These drives are psychic and physiological in origin. They are nothing with which adults can argue. Only the child can be the authority for what he feels. When the child has the feeling of security in his environment and trusts it, he can consciously develop the socialized behavior sought by the culture into which he is born. Those who do not experience this affection develop mechanisms by which they defend themselves against insecurity, fear, and anxiety.

Interestingly enough, every person wants to think of his behavior as normal, and it *is* normal for him in any situation, with the feelings he has. If it were to rain today, the weatherman could explain what combination of circumstances caused the rainfall. Weather is always normal to the weatherman. The same is true about behavior. There are causes behind behavior. The behavior of a boy is always normal to that boy.

From this point of view, a boy with a problem is not to be considered as bad, even though his behavior is highly undesirable from a social point of view. Rather, he is a person who is responding to a situation with feelings which he has not been able to escape or master. He is responding to the situation in the only way he can, for that is the way the situation appears to him. He will be able to behave differently only when he sees and feels it differently.

Those who approach the boy having this problem with an attitude of "I'll teach him a lesson!" only reinforce his feeling that everyone is against him. A child who feels alone has little chance of winning. The very time when the child is most unlovable is usually the time he is most in need of love. All studies reveal a close relationship between the child's social and emotional growth and these feelings on the part of the parents.

The importance of the boy's feelings in behavior

A generation ago, adults were telling youth, "*Can't* never did anything." Children in kindergarten today love the story of the little engine, "I Think I Can." This shift from outer exhortation to the importance of feelings on the inside of the child is in line with the newer insight into the importance of how a child feels. To feel able to read, rather than to be able to read, is the beginning of reading. To have reason to do, not to have the command to do, is a cause for action.

Evidence of the importance of these feelings has been experienced by every person who has set a continuous series of tasks before a child and insisted on their performance, when the child felt they were beyond his ability. It has been found not only that the child fails to perform the tasks, but that he retreats often to a level below his present performance, to a place where he can feel secure.

Progression of feeling in healthy personality growth

There is a healthy, orderly progression in the development of feeling toward himself, his world, and people, just as there is a sequence in growth. Each feeling tends to form a foundation on which the next can develop. Rather than being points which are passed and are no longer part of the person, they are more like a framework supporting the personality. Each one is a feeling that is needed continuously throughout life, though the form or the source may change according to the stage of development. The removal of any supporting part of the structure brings the personality tumbling down to that level. Here is the sequential development.

1. The foundation of this feeling structure is a sense of security—in the universe. This is developed in the earliest years, primarily by the way in which the child's physical and affectional needs are satisfied. From the care of his physical needs, the child develops the feeling that the world is dependable, that it can be trusted. From satisfying his emotional needs, he develops a feeling of personal worth. The parents control this life line through which he develops his relationship to the world about him. Feeling secure in his environment, he is ready to learn. Later in childhood, he must feel acceptable to other adults as well as to his parents. In adolescence, acceptance must come from one's own crowd, too.

2. Secure in this feeling of trust and personal worth, the boy begins to build a self-image, an image of himself as a separate, distinct individual, a person with a mind and a will of his own. Feeling secure, he directs himself toward his world, testing it and himself at the same time. He discovers the nature of the world, as distinguished from himself, and finds his limits of operation. He begins to feel able to cope with his environment and learns how to get the help of others when he needs it.

3. The third of these primary life relationships, the feeling that should be established in the early years (five or under) is the feeling that the child is able to do things. Believing himself to be worthy and independent, he will begin to fashion himself after those about him. It is a great period of imitative activities and continuous action, a period of plans and ideas. He is developing a feeling that he can act for himself.

4. The early school days provide the first big opportunity for the child to compare himself with others like himself. Building upon the first three achievements and relying upon them to support him, his feeling able to do things leads him to

the acquiring of many skills in school or in play. It is a period of tremendous development in skills and of a desire to be as competent as those about him. He begins to need their approval as well as the approval of adults. As long as he feels able to meet situations, he will learn and progress. The lower his feeling is of security, independence, and ability to do things, the quicker he reaches the place where he flees from life rather than face it. As long as he feels loved, he will learn; as soon as he feels fear, he will flee. And when he flees from life, he will not stop until he arrives at a place where he feels secure. From this new-found security he will begin to build again.

5. In early adolescence, the boy becomes especially conscious of his self again. He begins to feel the pressure of society demanding that he be competent and able to contribute to life. There are periods of power, followed by periods of questioning. He wants to face life but he wonders if he has what it takes. This period is not easy for either adults or teenagers, but this is the battleground for the birth of a man. Adults will need to be understanding and to support him in his struggle for self-acceptance as he is, and his feeling that with what he is, he can play his role as an adult.

6. Having won this battle of independence for the second time, he now begins to feel himself a part of all his society and community in a new way. He can share intimately in their ideals, hopes, and friendships. He has achieved the emotional maturity on which rich fellowship and life partnership can be successfully erected. Having found himself through the love of others, he is now able to give love back to the world. He will be able to give it, not only to his life partner, but generously for all of life. He has discovered the master key to living.

This kind of achievement in feelings toward life is not produced on an assembly line even though it is progressive. It is produced in intimate, loving living, where people trust one another and where the strengths of the family support one another. This does not imply that parents need to be perfect. They will and can make many mistakes—all but the one of failing to make certain that their son is aware of how much they love him.

Feelings are on the inside. They are the forces that create or cripple the healthy personality. Basic to growth and character formation is the need to be loved. Children can not devote themselves to anything else until that need is satisfied. Being satisfied, they are free to grow and to learn. Through devious ways of trading love for love, they eventually arrive at the place where they can give love whether it is returned or not.

CHAPTER 10

How to Influence a Boy's Behavior

The editor of a small-town paper covered the police department on a day when the regular reporter was ill. He was so alarmed at the number of minor delinquencies against property recorded in the preceding twenty-four hours that he directed his leading editorial toward this problem. After expressing concern over the situation, he proposed his solution. Every father in the community was to take his son into the parlor and have a heart-to-heart talk with him about the value of private property. Is that the solution to the problem?

It is desirable for fathers and sons to be on such terms that they have frequent occasions when they can share their values with one another verbally. Undoubtedly, however, all boys who commit these pranks have full knowledge of their father's value systems. They have learned this through the day-by-day experiences of living in the family. Talking to people must rank very low as a means of getting people to change their ways. A wag once said, "People give advice so readily because it is so easy and cheap." If talking to people made them better, this world would be well nigh perfect, for everyone has endured or suffered this method since time began. The other traditional methods of producing change seem equally weak.

The heart-to-heart talk, giving advice, exhortation, pleading shame, punishment, and signing a pledge, all tend to produce more feelings of guilt or anxiety than change in behavior.

Why do boys behave as they do? What are the more effective means of influencing change, if that is what is desired?

The point has been made that there are basic, positive feelings that the boy must have toward the world if he is to grow, and these come first. Having these feelings, the boy will still come into many conflicts with his environment and will need help, understanding, and patience, as well as firm and consistent treatment from those about him.

Outside commands will be of little help to children who are overtimid, who are worried, who tend to blame others for their failures, who continually tell lies, who balk at taking responsibility, who demand constant attention, or give other evidences of fleeing from life or fighting it. Such children need special attention and help, for these are evidences of serious emotional difficulty. They probably need help from some specialist in the field.

This chapter is not concerned with the type of difficulties suggested in the preceding paragraph. It is concerned with the way adults help growing children resolve the problems they face in their environment.

Part of the consideration will be given to problems which adults have and part to problems which children have.

The biggest problem facing adults is adjusting the degree of perfection they expect from a child to the realities of the situation. Most adults have quite a clear picture of the kind of behavior they expect from their child. Often it is a blend of their dreams and their hopes, with little attention to the complex situations in which boys can get involved today, or the memory of the things the parents did in their own childhood.

The truth is that children, yes, even children who are loved, will misbehave. They will probably bully, cheat, lie, engage in sex play, defy authorities, and do many of the things that disturb adults. If they did not, they would hardly be normal.

Probably most children have had moments when their behavior would have been considered delinquent if it had been known at that time. Fortunately, adults catch only glimpses of a child's behavior when he gets old enough to play about the neighborhood or go to school. If parents knew everything their children did, they would probably become quite concerned—just as their parents would have been concerned about them. Much of this behavior, however, is an extension of play, a part of the testing of their daring or of their world or of a situation beyond their experience. This is especially true of the boy in childhood.

With the adolescent, this behavior usually occurs in a group situation where members of his own age group are involved. These boys or youth will need help in gaining understanding of the effects of their actions and of better ways to achieve the purposes they had in mind. They should not be excused from facing the consequences of their actions, but they should face them with the support of those about them. These situations, however, are usually insufficient cause for deep concern. It is only when there is repetition of the same kinds of problems or when the motives that prompt the action seem to be unsocial that adults should begin to seek further for causes. It is a healthier situation when adults find situations where they can commend boys or youth on the fine things they are doing, rather than to be probing for causes of unsatisfactory behavior which they have witnessed.

Another responsibility facing adults is to create a consistent plan of living so the boy will have some clear picture of what is expected of him. This involves more than the setting of an example by the adults about him, powerful as example is. It means thoughtfully established limits of freedom, consistently followed when the boy is small, development of rules and regulations in the essential areas of living in boyhood, and the creation of broad principles of action for middle and late adolescence. The limits of freedom are established by adults only, on the basis of what he seems able to handle and support. The rules and regulations are developed within the family by all its members. The principles are a formulation by family and outside groups, based on experience.

Within this plan of living, the boy can always know which of his acts will bring approval and which disapproval. He needs this consistent framework for his happiest growth. He does not have the experience to handle freedom when he is small. He should be progressively prepared to handle freedom so that he can take over the control of his life gradually and be prepared for the independence which he will demand in later adolescence and which the community will expect of him as a young adult.

Although there are limits of freedom and rules, even principles, which are applied to situations consistently and firmly, the cause of the discipline should continue to reside in the situation, not in the adult. This is where it is at the start, but harsh application of rules or principles—as though one were enjoying seeing the victim squirm—can cause the child to project the cause of pain or unhappiness away from the situation onto the adult. Adults can be consistent and firm, yet remain friendly. This friendliness will override many of the mistakes which all adults make in the application of discipline. Even rules can bend, for situations are not always the same. Firmness does not mean rigidity. Rigidity and strictness only tend to produce more problems.

Another major responsibility of adults is to be clear as to what they are trying to accomplish, what their goals are as they deal with these problems. These goals must be projected on the basis of an understanding of behavior and an understanding of how they can be effective in influencing it. These goals must also be adjusted in terms of the boy, his age, his past behavior, and the cultural pattern in which he lives. These statements are descriptive of the goals adults are seeking for their boys:

To provide opportunities for a boy to work off his hostilities without adding to the problem situation.

To help a boy increase his ability to handle freedom or independence through progressive experience with it.

To help a boy achieve more competence in the handling of his own life through a more sensitive understanding of his behavior in relation to others.

To help a boy become willing and able to accept responsibility for his own life and to be helpful to those about him.

These goals grow out of the understanding of behavior as purposive, as being an expression of deep inner drives and feelings concerned with the preservation of his body and his ego. Goodness, therefore, cannot be added from the outside or commanded into existence.

Power over a boy cannot substitute for his own inner controls. Adults soon discover that changes in the boy need to be accompanied by changes in themselves, both in their attitude toward him and in their behavior. They accept the idea that boys do have periods when they are bothered by fears, angers, and worries, and they need opportunities to work them off rather than suppress them. Finally, they know that the security of adults can never be threatened by a boy's behavior, but only by their own. Boys may strike out at adults in defense of their own self-image, but adults need not become anxious. They are the last persons boys want to alienate. Boys need them and must have them for their own security.

There is no magic wand or set of rules through which these goals can be achieved, but there are ways of dealing with boys in their problem moments that are more productive than others. Some specifics are suggested here; many more will appear throughout the book whenever a basic problem is discussed.

How adults can encourage desirable behavior

Adults can try to understand what boys are trying to do. Because of their experience, they can make it possible for boys to achieve their goals, often worthy in themselves, in ways that are socially satisfying. They need to take the child's point of view into consideration, see his goal and his motives, before jumping to conclusions.

An irate executive literally dragged a nine-year-old boy into his office and accused him of trying to tear the expensive side lights off the entry to the building. The little fellow was so frightened and so threatened that he could not utter a word in explanation or defense. An associate gave the boy time to quiet down and then learned from him that a group of them had been playing "tag," the all-American game for boys of this age. It seemed that a fellow could be tagged if his feet were touching the ground. "Golly, Mister," he said, "I didn't want to hurt the light but what would you have done if two guys were coming at you and you had nothing to get hold of to pull your feet up in the air?" It didn't take long for this associate to suggest a better place to play and to point out the importance of lights in the building.

In a community without much play space, the boys were breaking street lights until several dads purchased a basketball goal and helped them attach it to the side of a house. The breaking of street lights stopped.

Adults can provide opportunities for boys to develop skills or abilities so that their behavior is more satisfying to them.

A father who was always berating his son for round shoulders put a bar in his backyard. The son developed the muscles and the pride in his body that made him want to walk erectly. The mother who was fearful of the nearby lake provided opportunities for swimming instruction so that her fears would not need to limit the boy's activities. The neighborhood gang was organized into a club so that the boys could have constructive use of their leisure time.

Adults can encourage youth to increase their competence and their confidence in themselves in these ways:

Help boys like themselves. A club composed mostly of problem boys was led by their leader to try doing something helpful in school rather than to get their recognition through roughhouse play. Their work in the cafeteria carrying trays for little children was noticed by the principal. He called the group into the office to commend them and later gave them public recognition. This incident marked the turn in their attitude toward the school.

Allow boys to commit mistakes without losing their self-respect; help them to grow beyond errors. Two boys were involved in separate auto accidents. One father deprived the boy of the car for six months. The other father was concerned, but recognized that adults have accidents, too. He and the boy discussed what had happened, how it might have been avoided, or such possibilities reduced, and they worked out a way to have the car fixed.

Encourage growing skill. The recital of the first-year class in band instruments may not have been an artistic thrill, but father and mother both attended; and they celebrated that evening by having dinner in the dining room with all their son's favorite foods.

Permit freedom to make some important decisions and to be responsible for them. The clothes budget for the adolescent was divided with one-half in the boy's account and one-half in his mother's account. If he wanted a new sweater or other clothing, and his mother agreed that he needed it, he could pick it out and each paid half. If his mother did not feel he needed it, he could still buy it, but the entire amount came from the boy's account.

Adults can provide opportunities for a boy to work off his hostilities. The father who can smile and tell his son that there are times when he would be glad to sell him for a bag of peanuts frees his son to acknowledge that sometimes he feels dad is not so hot either, without feeling guilty. The small child needs opportunities to draw and scribble or hammer and bang, to make sand pies and mess them up, or to pile blocks and knock them down.

A camp staged a big ceremony and burned the camp grouch in which everyone had buried their hates during the day. He burned with Roman candles shooting out of his head and arms while young Indians danced war dances around the circle.

Adults can restrict a boy, yet let him know he is still loved.

The family had a rule that any member who would not be able to return home at about the hour they had indicated would telephone and report when they could be expected. Parents and children abided by the same rule. John, aged thirteen, had failed to follow the rule for two consecutive Friday nights. As a result, he was not permitted to leave the house on the third Friday night. Somehow, during that long evening, his mother found time to help him make a batch of fudge, and dad played his favorite card game with him for part of the evening.

Adults can provide opportunities for a boy to try his own ideas of right and wrong.

On the morning of a heavy snowfall, the mother had called her son extra early for school, because she knew the bus would not be on time, perhaps not even come at all. She made his favorite breakfast, then sent him off to school, on foot. About an hour later, he telephoned from school, saying that only about half of the students were in school, so he and three of his friends were going to leave school and go tobogganing. The mother almost wished she had let him stay in bed rather than calling him early and taking all the extra trouble with breakfast. However, she did not express these thoughts to him. She only said, "Well, John, you know how the family feels about school. You know the right thing to do. You'll have to make your own decision." John stayed in school. When he came home that evening, he remarked, "Gee, Mom, you sure made it tough for me this morning."

How adults often encourage undesirable behavior

Changing rules without the boy's knowledge; applying rules that do not apply; throwing all the rules at a boy because of one situation. A boy will respect rules so long as they are fair. When those who apply them are unfair, in his eyes, the rules cease to be valid. They are applied according to whim. He has no consistent way to judge his conduct, so he tries to evade.

Trying to shame a child into good behavior. Shaming a child is an attack on his self-respect. It makes him feel weaker rather than stronger.

Inflicting physical punishment unless one is convinced it is the best and only way to teach in a particular situation. Physical punishment, which is the hurting or the infliction of pain, is highly ineffective after the child has attained some ability to understand. After the pain is forgotten, the humiliation lingers. Few adults can remember physical punishment with any feeling that it was deserved or effective. Fear is hardly the path to a healthy personality.

A demonstration of power, emphasizing one's superb status. Displays of power by adults are demonstrations of insecurity rather than competence. Self-respect is accompanied by personal dignity and control. The younger child, who imitates, receives a faulty pattern and the older child develops hostilities.

Expressions or attitudes that indicate readiness to hate others. Slurring remarks about races or minority groups are an attack upon everyone's security. A healthy personality does not need scapegoats.

Attempts to suppress the boy's fears or anxieties. A boy cannot be kidded out of his feelings. It is better to acknowledge his fears as real to him, and help him find ways of dealing with them.

Referring again and again to past errors. Past mistakes are past. They should not be recalled again and again as a club over a boy's head or as a reason for depriving him of some privilege. He needs confidence in himself, not shame or humiliation, if he is to grow.

Threats. Threats of punishment induce lies and secrecy. Threats of "I won't love you if you do this" bind the youngster who believes it is true and disgusts those who see its infantile basis.

Comparison with others. Children resent this very much, especially if they are set in an unfavorable light. They feel it is unfair. It increases their insecurity. When they are compared as superior, they become haughty. If it is true, they don't need the comparison; they know it.

Absence of rules; keeping children afraid. Without some established limits of freedom, the child is subject to the whims of those about him. He is not able to predict the response of adults to his behavior. Firm, reasonable rules are a comfort for a child. There should not be so many that he is freed from all choices, but enough so that he does not feel the strain of continual choice. The child who is afraid feels alone and unworthy. His behavior will be an expression of this kind of personality.

In these negative ways of dealing with a child, the boy is either being exploited to satisfy the emotional demands of the adults about him or he is having the door opened for him to try these negative patterns upon those about him. Behavior which tends to devour others will always be resisted. Behavior which supports or develops the potential in others will always be welcome.

CHAPTER 11

How a Boy Develops in Infancy (Birth Through Age 2)

Prelude

Meet the boss. This is the boy who can't use words but has every adult in the house rushing to serve him. Dignified individuals resort to baby talk and make faces that probably frighten him, but the attention pleases his parents. Wonder and admiration are read into every action. "Our baby did . . ." dominates the table conversation. He may look a little odd to others, but to the family he is the most beautiful child in the world.

Father beams with pride when others fondle his heir, but wears the anxious, uncomfortable look of one holding expensive china when baby son is in his arms. To him, the first six months are a dead loss. He longs for the day he can rough it up a bit. For mother, they are days of endless chores and steps. Baby falls asleep a split second before she is about to collapse—and then he looks so sweet—the little darling.

It's both frightening and wonderful, but above all, a great joy.

The world of infancy

The world of the infant is one of insecurity and struggle for comfort and survival, shifting to acquaintance with people and their No's.

Birth itself is possibly the greatest shock the human organism is ever called upon to withstand. Projected suddenly into the world from the warm, protected, sustaining environment of his mother's body, the infant must adjust suddenly to tremendous changes if he is to survive. It is no wonder he greets life with a cry. This sound, which is so welcome to those about him, represents the beginning of his reorganization to a world totally foreign to him. It is "threatening" not only to the person he is to become, but to his very survival. He meets these "threats" daily and his cries are his protests against his discomfort. As he begins to associate comfort with the response he secures, they become his language. The "cry," however, most nearly pictures the first world of the infant. How different this is from the sweet, comfortable world most adults picture for him.

Infancy is also the period of acquaintance with people. There are not many people, mostly those of his intimate family, especially Mother. At first he appears to be the ruler of these people. He is the king; those about him, his slaves. He demands what he wants, expects to get it and usually does. Slowly he begins to sense his dependency upon the help and affection of those about him. He needs them so much that he becomes possessive.

As he begins to toddle about, these people about him begin to change. The adults who had previously answered his commands pay less attention to his orders now. They begin giving commands and expecting him to respond. The world which had existed *for* him now seeks to control him. He meets *No, mustn't, stop,* in a constant barrage. If he does not heed these warnings, he often suffers pain.

He likes to play with squeaky toys, stuffed animals, blocks, and push-and-pull toys. He loves to play in sand and water. He likes to have adults play with him, and often enjoys rough horseplay (which shouldn't exceed the point where it is fun for him).

The world of the infant and the toddler is very small, but he has so much to master. His world is his mother, the family, and his home. He is usually in contact with at least one of these three. He will have to gain his security and begin his growth in this world.

Developmental tasks of infancy

The most important task of the infant and the toddler is to establish himself as a separate, distinct individual and to learn how to live with others in the family. This is a sizable task, for he has no previous experience to guide him. He must learn everything from the beginning. Along with this living satisfactorily with the persons in his world are other tasks to be accomplished if he is to be prepared for early childhood. Those needing major attention have an asterisk (*) before the numeral.

*1. *Accepting himself as satisfactory to those about him.* The boy in infancy and in toddler days will begin his first picture of himself as a person. This feeling toward and about himself is the foundation of much of his behavior. The only way he can feel about himself is the way those about him seem to feel toward him. If people play with him, talk to him, cuddle him, if those about him are happy, he will feel that they care, that he is loved, that he is satisfactory.

He is uncanny in his ability to sense the feelings of others toward him. If he feels unwanted, unsatisfactory, rejected, he will be deeply hurt and will feel that he is not of much value. Under these conditions it will be almost impossible for him to have the courage to grow. He cannot feel strong outside if he does not feel strong inside.

*2. *Being able to respond to love.* The ability to respond to love requires a freedom of the individual. To be outgoing, the infant and toddler must be above the need for the defense of self. The baby can be free and outgoing when he feels secure. This first security comes from the experience he has with his physical needs being cared for. If he finds his needs being met when he is uncomfortable, he develops a feeling that this world is dependable, that it can be trusted.

This dependability is important. He must know that he can depend on those around him, that he can depend on them with no strings attached. At times he tests it; he should not be able to find limits. He should always feel that he has support. It can be a helping hand, a smile, or play, but it will need to be adequate to his need.

*3. *Developing an awareness of individuality and dependency*. The infant or the toddler who has a well-established feeling that the universe is friendly begins to assert himself and becomes aware of himself as a separate, autonomous person, one who has separate, independent existence.

Being a separate person soon makes him aware of his dependency. He finds himself running into an endless series of restraining commands. He is learning his limits of freedom. He must learn what is permitted and what is not.

What is to be permitted and what is not to be permitted should be reasonably and firmly established. It should be done in ways that encourage him to keep moving toward independence.

4. *Enjoying play with Mother and those of the immediate family*. The first play of the infant and the toddler is with his mother and he enjoys it immeasurably. Others of the family circle who are around him often are able to enter into play, but no one has the center of his attention as much as the one who cares for him.

He will play near other children but he does not play with them. If he wants what other children have, he grabs it. He does not know how to share. Toys should be provided for each child.

*5. *Growing with accompanying big-muscle development.* The early life of the infant and toddler is a period of rapid growth and he faces the problem of developing co-ordination of mind and body. It is a period of large-muscle activity, developing ability to grasp objects, to get around, to get what he wants. These skills develop naturally when the body is ready, but some play or celebration will make them satisfying. This activity should be encouraged with appropriate objects, for it helps him differentiate himself from his environment.

This body development moves from the upper portion of the body toward the lower, and eventually his muscles and his feelings will make him ready for walking. There is nothing parents can do to hurry this period. When he is ready, he will begin to pull himself up, to stand, and finally to have equilibrium and walk. This is the time when well-fitting shoes are essential. Walking toys that make noise are favorites.

6. *Being able to approve his own human nature.* The infant and toddler needs to feel that everything about himself is acceptable. No part of his body should be considered dirty or undesirable. His touching of his genitals during a bath can hardly be avoided; his little hand reaches just that far. Certainly this is not the time to slap his hand and say "naughty." The bath can be continued naturally and the hand involved with something else if the adult is concerned. The child should feel that every part of his body is satisfactory.

*7. *Adjusting to beginning cultural expectancies.* The infant and toddler who feels the love of his parents, will be able to respond to them when they begin to demand of him that he conform to the expectancies of the culture of which he is a part. The power that he enjoyed in his early months soon begins to give way and he finds a confusing array of demands placed upon him. He discovers that instead of being king, he is dependent on those about him. He saves his ego by identifying with those about him who make him feel of worth to them. In order to continue this feeling of worth to them, he seeks to do the things that make them happy. As long as these demands seem reasonable, he will respond successfully. In this spirit he responds to the cultural plan of eating, of being clean, of leaving something alone.

Eating is so natural that it is hard to conceive of its becoming a battle, yet this often happens. A positive, confident attitude by those who feed him is most important. Eating should be fun. These are days when he will want to help himself, so let him enjoy this thrill.

Toilet training is different. This provides the child with his first chance of being defiant and holding back. If he feels happy toward life, he will learn these new habits willingly and with them develop a healthy attitude toward authority. Toilet training accompanied by impatience, harsh treatment, or punishment may make the child stubborn and give him little reason to co-operate. Many child specialists believe that negative character traits that exist through life may be traced to badly managed toilet training. In a happy atmosphere, children become willing to co-operate, to be generous, to be givers; in an unhappy atmosphere, they devise ways of holding back, of defying, of being stingy. How he responds at this time will affect his relations with people throughout his life; and the parent's attitude will color his response.

8. *Developing sounds and beginning communication.* Crying is the infant's first language. Spontaneous vocalization comes next. Words follow soon after. He will not learn to talk unless someone talks to him. Phrases follow words, sentences follow phrases. He will play with sounds naturally, but communication with words is learned from those about him.

9. *Being eager to touch and feel things in his environment.* The toddler is getting into an action period and it is good for him to touch and handle the things in his environment. If some things are valuable, they can be set out of his way for a while. He needs to develop some acquaintance with and mastery of the world in which he lives.

*10. *Adjusting to adult restrictions.* As the toddler begins to move more and more about the house, he runs into more and more restrictions. These are imposed upon him by adults upon whom he depends. If he feels that he is satisfactory to them, he will not feel a need to fight in defense of his emerging individuality. Under these conditions he is free to grow and he will seek their approval of his acts. This will mean the accepting of their restrictions.

Major responsibilities of adults with boys in infancy and with toddlers

The major responsibilities of adults in the life of the infant or the toddler are to give him a sense of security in his world and to help him establish himself as a person.

Adults can help him gain a sense of security. In his days of infancy, the boy cannot be overvalued. In his helplessness he tends to draw upon the completeness of those around him for his own sense of being wanted and being acceptable to them. He will be a tyrant in his demands. His physical needs cannot endure frustrations. Filling these needs will not spoil him. It will assure him that the world is a good place. It can be trusted. But these are not enough. He must be held, played with, talked to, enjoyed, and spontaneously loved if he is to grow and become loving himself.

Moving from being completely helpless, demanding and receiving, toward becoming self-sufficient, co-operating and giving, involves a long period of growing up, but these early days are among the most important. Even though the boy does not remember all the experiences, they form the foundation of the way he feels about people and the way he will eventually get along with them.

The unthinking love which is so generous, so natural, and so beneficial in the early days must be supported by understanding as the infant grows. The early growth is thrilling. At first it is measured in ounces, then pounds and inches. It will be according to the boy's own pace. Friends and neighbors may talk about how their son sat up at so many weeks old, or walked in so many months. They do not set the pattern for this new life. Each child has his own pace. The real cue to his readiness for these achievements will be when he starts to do them himself.

Physical growth, however, is not the only growth occurring. He is growing in his feelings about himself and those in the world about him. He has hardly established confidence in the dependability of his world before the pressures of the culture into which he was born begin to press in upon him. It has probably started with his feeding schedule. Periods are being lengthened between feedings and he is being moved toward three meals a day. He is being prepared to live as a member of a family where others have rights and need freedoms, too.

Adults can help him establish himself as a person. A healthy, loved toddler will be happy. It is completely desirable for him to be a satisfied child. Actually it is hard to spoil him if parents take his learning cues from him. When he wants to do things by himself, he should be encouraged. Praise and celebrations of success make him feel strong enough to move ahead. It is these inner feelings about himself that are the keys to action. Initiative cannot be commanded, so when it appears it should be celebrated. It need not be displayed with the best china but he will have no objection to having blocks, spools, or pans as the objects to pound, pile, or throw. These constructive growth signs can always be directed toward constructive opportunities.

Toddling days are not the days for talking things over with him or asking him to do things. These are days for action. Doing things with him and showing him how they are done are the ways to get co-operation. It is always necessary to pace oneself to his feeling. When he feels like a little child, he should be treated that way. When he acts like a big boy, he needs the big boy treatment. Co-operating with him will not spoil him. It is when adults deal with him in relation to *their* feelings rather than *his* that he is in greatest danger of being spoiled or exploited.

CHAPTER 12

How a Boy Develops in Early Childhood (Ages 3-4-5)

Prelude

"Me and My Shadow" is the parents' theme song during early childhood. The boy in this period is continually underfoot in his play or in his eagerness to help. These are the days of the human question mark and the "hot-rod kid" of the tricycle. Puddles were made to sit in and clothes get dirty—as if the family owned the laundry. He imitates his parents in his play and wears them out with his energy. It is a race between one's endurance and the start of his school days.

The world of early childhood

The world of early childhood is an exciting adventure of self-assertion and acquaintance with and mastery of the child's surroundings, constantly being limited by adults. It is also the world in which his conscience begins to develop.

By early childhood, the boy has discovered how trustworthy his world is, and he has discovered that he is a separate individual of some standing.

He is building a self-image from his experience with the world. If he feels that he is satisfactory, he will not need to defend himself and he will not have the urge to hostile expressions.

With these ideas of his world and himself, he plunges into getting better acquainted with his world and trying to win mastery over it. Adventure is on every side of him. The world is new and exciting. He wants to feel, handle, test everything. He gets so busy and so consumed with these opportunities that he greets adults with No. Little wonder, for that is the word he had been hearing most from them. He does not seem to mean No. It's just that he is too busy to be bothered, and he trusts his environment. He's a boy in a new toy shop. There's too much to see or to experiment with, but he's going to give it a healthy try.

These are the days of toy telephones, trucks, tractors, the nonelectric train, building blocks, and drums. He enjoys being on the go. Arm, leg, and trunk muscles are seldom still. Tricycles ("three-wheelers" or "three-wheeled bikes") become great fun. He loves playing in sand and water. He can't walk around a water puddle; he wants to be right in the middle of it. He likes to play with a blackboard, large crayons, paints, modeling clay, big paper boxes, small table and chairs.

He wants to explore. He loves picnics and trips to the zoo. He likes noise. He likes to hear his voice. He likes slapstick, big movement humor, like a pillow fight. He enjoys make-believe play, imitating adult activities. Fairy stories are enjoyed. Good stories are welcomed. Story and music records are popular. He wants his favorite stories over and over again.

He enjoys other children and begins to recognize their skills, but play is often parallel rather than with them. He asserts his individualism by grabbing things from them if he desires them. Most of this period can be characterized by a mild sort of rivalry. If one child pleases an adult, the other child will do the same thing because he wants the adults to approve him too. He may become aggressive or cry if his beloved nursery teacher fails to notice him. Two children occasionally pair off alone and play fairly well, but the introduction of a third person stimulates the rivalry again. The boy always wants to appear at best advantage. By the age of five, however, he will begin to enjoy co-operative play.

He loves his family but demands his right to do things by himself—such as buttoning his clothes, feeding himself, pouring his milk—and he often becomes impatient of his naturally gradual achievement. Mother's approval is especially important to him and he will often do things to seek her favor. She is in almost hourly attendance upon his wants; and it is Mother who comforts him when he is hurt. He is often envious of attentions she shows Father or his brothers and sisters, and will reveal his resentment in acts of "misbehavior" that can be explained in no other way.

Nonetheless, both parents seem all-powerful to him. In his great dependency on them, he is often concerned about losing them or their losing him. He is extremely possessive of them.

Dad's star begins to rise in relation to his son. The boy has begun to identify himself as male, both from his recognition of physical and sexual differences and from attitudes expressed consciously or unconsciously by other children and older people. (Ever hear Mom tell Dad and Sonny, "You men come here!") This is his first move toward a masculine role, which will often express itself in amusing imitation of Dad. These are the days when he begins to want to help his father in work around the yard, or to go on expeditions to the store or park with him.

Adults open many new opportunities for him to venture into his world but they always seem to limit his exploration, or his fun. Having become dependent upon them, he identifies with them to save his ego. Now these limitations imposed upon him become his limitations. He begins to build them into a pattern for himself. It becomes a conscience that limits him even when adults are not around him. Right at the time when he is eager to explore and conquer, an inner No begins to operate. It can't bother much now, for there are so many adventures and everything is his world. Property has no owners yet.

The world of early childhood is not very large. It includes the neighborhood, the people in it or those who enter it.

Developmental tasks of early childhood

In early childhood the tasks needing attention, if the boy is to move forward eagerly to the next stage of life, center around his exploration of his world, the establishment of relationships with those about him, and a more complete discovery of himself.

The list that follows may seem formidable for the little lad in early childhood, but the tasks are elementary and move along easily if he has acquired the feeling that he is satisfactory to those about him. Those needing major attention have an asterisk (*) before the numeral. All the tasks in this section are considered major tasks.

*1. *Accepting himself as a separate, distinct individual of worth.* The boy in early childhood must feel that human nature is worthy of respect. He judges this by the respect that is shown to him and the dignity with which human beings near him handle themselves. He needs to feel able to show his feelings, not that they are always right but that human nature is good more often than bad. As he gains confidence in his freedom to test and explore his world, he develops a clearer picture of himself as a separate, distinct person with abilities and worth.

*2. *Having ability to show affection toward others.* This world on which the boy depends so desperately in early childhood is often shaken by the birth of a new baby in the home. The family tends to get so busy with the new member that a boy may feel forgotten. He cannot be expected to take this lying down. Though this may be the time when he must give up being the baby, he must be given some other ego-satisfying role, or it will be more than he can take. He cannot give up his personal demands because of his real dependency. If he is old enough to be a partner in planning for the arrival or to have extra privileges, he can be happy. If he is still a little boy, he must not be forgotten. He must feel that his world is secure, that he is satisfactory, if he is to be outgoing and friendly to others.

*3. *Developing a sense of physical independence within a framework of dependency.* The boy in early childhood needs trust in his world and an increasing awareness of himself if he is to feel in a mood to test his environment. He wants to liberate himself from the feeling of dependence at the same time that he wants to be sure that he can depend on those about him. He wants both the independence of being grown, and the dependence of being small.

He will be eagerly exploring, trying his own way, and using his new skills. He needs this experience if he is to grow toward a feeling of independence. This independence must be earned and felt from within.

The child that feels free and able to move into the world, and finds it satisfying, is well started toward a pattern of maturity. He will like to do things for himself, or for others. This will take more time but it helps him reach toward independence. He is primarily engaged in how to live with others and how to live in our kind of world.

*4. *Enjoying play in the company of others.* These days in early childhood will be his first big encounter with other children like himself. While he will not play with them very much, he will be drawn naturally to them and should enjoy having them around. The play will be parallel play at the beginning of the period, gradually shifting to some play with them toward the end of early childhood. Two children play together fairly well, but three find it much more difficult. When adults are nearby, the flow tends to go from child to adult. Nursery school teachers report some beginnings of sharing, co-operation, and sympathy, but much of the play is individual or in competition with others. The child shows some definite choice in friends.

*5. *Becoming aware of sex differences and adjusting to the cultural pattern of sex differences.* The boy in early childhood needs to be aware of sex differences as a part of learning his sex role. He usually notices these differences and asks about them. He should receive unhesitant, unembarrassed, matter-of-fact answers. Some families bathe and toilet together as a natural, healthy way of teaching these differences and inculcating the attitude that all parts of our bodies are good and clean and wholesome. Children of this age often play at doctor, nurse, mother or father, as a part of imitating adult life. Handling of genitals is common. Some sex exploration and masturbation occurs. These pass naturally if adults do not get excited. More play equipment or opportunities will divert the boy's attention unless he uses masturbation as a means of self-love to fill a need for parental affection and attention he feels is lacking; and secretiveness and failure to answer his sex questions may only lead to further sex exploration with other children.

Children of this age ask questions about everything. They will undoubtedly include questions about the origin of babies. These questions should be answered simply and as easily as other questions the boy may ask.

*6. *Growing, with continuing development of big-muscle skills and motor abilities.* The boy in early childhood needs a wide variety of large-muscle activity that will develop muscles of shoulders, arms, trunk, and legs. He will want opportunities to climb, swing, pound nails, ride his "bike" or scooter. He will enjoy running, jumping, galloping, dodging, swimming or play in water. He can understand restrictions on throwing stones and sticks, but may forget them in the excitement of play.

*7. *Continuing his achievements in elementary cultural patterns of physical care.* Boys in early childhood face many cultural patterns in eating, bathing, toilet care, dressing, washing, and resting, related to their physical health and body care, that they must continue to accept if they are to be happy. The acceptance of these patterns from their family depends upon their feeling of trust in the world and security in the family. Feeling accepted and approved by the family, they identify with them and accept their patterns of life.

Boys who respond to the cultural training of their parents will try to establish this same relationship with other adults—if these adults give them the same sense of security that they feel in their home. A rejected child of 3, 4, or 5 can hardly excel enough in any situation to compensate for this lack of security.

*8. *Developing initiative and language communication.* The boy in early childhood needs to try his wings. He wants to help himself, to try out his own ideas, to make decisions. He can almost dress himself, clean up his room after a fashion, bathe himself, feed himself, and help with household tasks. He wants more than this, however. He wants to try his own ideas. He will turn his "bike" over to make an airplane. He will take large cardboard boxes and have a castle. These are days of great enterprise and vigorous learning. Adults can provide materials and listen to his stories.

These are the big days of language, too. Talking with him and reading stories will help him develop new skill with words.

*9. *Extending his acquaintance with his environment.* The boy in early childhood is having many firsthand contacts with his world. He should be privileged to see, to feel, to handle, to manipulate everything that is possible without harm to himself or the objects. This is a period for contact with fundamental elements of dirt, water, sand, wood, and the like. Mechanical devices can come later. Family trips and picnics are desirable, too.

*10. *Accepting controls from others—beginning some control from a developing conscience.* A conscience develops in the boy in early childhood as the patterns of his family and their culture get incorporated into his own thinking. He begins to know what his parents expect of him and what brings their approval and disapproval. He incorporates their ideas into his thinking and begins to develop his own inner sense of how he should act—his conscience.

Acceptance of outer and inner controls rests on an assurance of worth and security. He can take correction of his actions if he is sure he is still acceptable as a person.

Major responsibilities of adults with boys in early childhood

The major responsibilities of the adults in the life of the boy in early childhood are to give him the support he needs as he moves out to establish his first big relationships with his world and the people in it, and to encourage him in his attempts to try his own ideas.

Adults can encourage his feeling of security and approval. Most of the big tasks of this period depend upon the feeling of security and trust the boy feels in his world. Unless he feels that he is satisfactory, that he is wanted, he will not have the courage to step out and meet life, or to accept the patterns of adults which are so essential for the development of his cultural pattern and his conscience.

Their approval will not be hard to give if adults will remember that this is the boy's first tussle with the larger world—and appreciate the size of the task. They should also remember that the boy is not trying to displease adults. He desperately needs their support. He will not alienate himself from them. His actions at this age are not defiance; they are his attempts to distinguish himself from things, to become a distinct individual, and to grapple with life.

In his days of early childhood, he goes through a No period that is common to all children. It seems to be part of the struggle to test himself to see if he is a real person who can assert himself. Parents who understand this are not alarmed. He will move through it as naturally as he did through creeping. Battling him on it tends to lengthen rather than to shorten it.

Even worse, it adds tension to a home, and small boys like a home where people seem relaxed and gay. It makes them feel that things are right in the world.

Many of the things that plague parents during the early childhood days will pass just like the No stage. Some sex curiosity is normal, and questions should be answered with simple statement of facts. If children take things which do not belong to them, these things should be returned, but few children know what belongs to them until they are five or six years of age. Big stories are the result of imagination and should not be treated as lies.

Stuttering is not a cause for direct concern with the boy in early childhood. Neither is thumb-sucking. When these habits occur they should not be dealt with directly, but the adults should examine the child's environment to see if they can locate the causes. Children cannot be shamed, scolded, or threatened out of this behavior. These efforts only make the behavior more necessary.

Discipline will be necessary occasionally when celebrations of success or approval have not produced the desired behavior. It cannot be administered every time the boy does something wrong but only when he does something where danger is involved or when positive, constructive suggestions have failed. It should be administered instantly, without dramatics, and completed. When it is over, the boy should be accepted back in the circle again. The incident is closed. Physical punishment, while still used in some groups, is rarely necessary. It should never be administered to relieve one's anger. Few adults can recall occasions when they think physical punishment was helpful.

Adults can encourage the boy to develop his initiative and acquaintance with the world. The boy will make many starts, many ventures into the world, then stop to see what adults think about it. If the start is in the wrong direction, adults might suggest another way and go along with him, but they should not make a habit of saying No. The boy needs to know the world and master the parts he meets. He should find contact with the world satisfying. To withdraw now would be to withdraw from his initial venture.

Fortunately he will not withdraw easily, but he will go much faster if the adults approve his ventures and praise him for his progress. He needs to know his world firsthand. An unknowing boy is usually afraid. That would be a poor start for any lad.

What the boy needs more than anything else in these early years is the feeling that he is thoroughly satisfactory. Upon this assurance he will feel eager to grow.

CHAPTER 13

How a Boy Develops in Middle Childhood (Ages 6-7-8)

Prelude

After a male baby has grown out of long clothes and triangles, and has acquired pants, freckles, and so much dirt that relatives dare not kiss it between meals, it becomes a boy. This description fits the boy of middle childhood, for this is the period of dirt, noise, questions, measles, and bumps. He can tire parents until they are tempted to write their Congressman, ship him to Grandmother, hang him on a nail, or tie him to a tree; but no matter how they may feel, none can resist him when he throws his loving arms about their neck.

The world of middle childhood

The world of middle childhood involves a boy's first big step outside his home and makes a new era in his living. Up till now his field of operation was the home, or within the sight of his home or parents. With the beginning of school, he has another center of operation and another set of adults in his life. In addition, he has a new crowd of contemporaries—most of whom are new to him. This change is as great for a boy as for an adult to move to a new town and start in a completely different job. This is a really new world, but if he were fortunate enough to live in a home where he has been loved and valued, as almost every boy is, he has accepted the values of his parents and found satisfaction in pleasing them. He carries this same pattern to school and, trying out the teacher and finding he is accepted by her, he wants to please her and accepts the standards of behavior she expects. Once he is sure of her, he has another center of security and the encounter with the rest of his world becomes possible.

The world of middle childhood expands more rapidly than any other a boy will ever experience unless it is going to college or into the armed services. Even these are hardly as great, for they occur when he has much more experience to cope with them. Starting to school is a step into the neighborhood community. From now on the steps into the world community will be only a matter of degree.

In this period a boy likes to please other adults outside his home, such as valued family friends. He likes to stand well with them. He begins to seek friends among his contemporaries and searches for those who satisfy his needs. Friendship at six years of age is of short duration, but lasting friendships are developing gradually. By eight years he can usually hold friends, and friendship becomes very important. By this age he can even share one of his friends with another.

Although boys and girls play together happily at these ages, by eight years boys of his own age become increasingly more important. Soon, his feeling of success or failure will depend more upon the esteem of his contemporaries than that of adults —even his parents. In this learning about friends and group living, he has many fights—all the way from name calling at six and seven to fist fights at eight, sometimes earlier. Yet boys who fight in the morning will be pals again in the afternoon.

He accepts persons of other races naturally and easily at these ages unless parents' prejudices interfere. Inevitable questions—many inspired by remarks of other children whose parents' prejudices have had their impact already—should be answered as objectively as those about sex: as no part of the body of the individual is inherently unwholesome, so too no part of the body of mankind is inherently unwholesome; all are sons and daughters of the same God, cherished equally by him. Now is the ideal time to establish such democratic and spiritual concepts.

A boy is still respectful of his parents' attitudes and values at this period. He boasts of his parents' wisdom and strength to his friends. He is still possessive of his parents, often revealing his rivalry with other brothers and sisters for parental affection and attention. He is often jealous if another baby arrives, or anyone else becomes a challenge to his position in the family. If he feels any real danger, he may begin to demand a show of love from his parents by reverting to infantile patterns of behavior. Thumb-sucking, nail-biting, even occasional toilet lapses or overt expressions of a desire to be a baby again, may occur. Similar tension behavior may reappear as he starts to school, indicating a lack of security and self-assurance.

Although seeking adult approval and admiration, the striving for independence that will eventually possess him is already evident. His use of shock words and actions increases. Regular routine may be opposed but his rebellion is not very real. He seems inattentive and somewhat messy. His room is usually in disorder. His clothes are worn in sloppy fashion. He appears especially immune to scoldings and commands, and he will lie to escape punishment.

But he will work hard if someone admires his work. He needs recognition and having gained some sense of money value, will want to be paid for chores; to him it symbolizes achievement and independence by adult standards. What he may do to achieve that wonderful feeling of being "able to do" and to win approval from others may range from reading at school, telling a story, or playing the piano to riding a bike, throwing a ball, or climbing a tree. His desire for self-sufficiency also extends to personal care, as in brushing his teeth or dressing himself.

His play activities involve simple games that stress individual activity; he begins to enjoy play in groups of six or eight, but will need an older leader to satisfy his demands for individual attention. Tag games are great favorites. Movement is necessary; noise, desirable. He recognizes the importance of rules in a game, but takes losing hard. By eight years, he begins to prefer distinctly "boy" games, such as baseball. He may, in fact, become the family authority on all the World Series baseball stars.

He will also spend hours playing in mud, wading in puddles, building a dam, a wagon, or an airplane, coasting downhill, falling in snow, or climbing a tree. Bikes (including "two-wheelers"), scooters, coaster wagons, sleds, skis, roller skates, and playground equipment satisfy his need for speed and for big-muscle development. He wants realism in toys—fire engines that clang, locomotives that smoke. He enjoys construction sets, kites, and simple electrical toys.

He gets fun out of things that appear simple to adults. His pockets are miniature museums. He collects, barters or exchanges many things. This is the time for first pets—hamster, rabbit, dog, cat, snake, frog, toad, lizard, mouse—anything alive that needs his care.

Dramatic play reveals his inner life. It centers around playing mother, father, teacher, and doctor at the beginning of this period, and moves toward "cops and robbers" and "cowboys and Indians" of the eight-year-old. Television, radio, and comics are great favorites. He prefers Western or adventure plots involving faraway places and people. Slapstick humor gets his vote.

The distinctive part of the world of middle childhood is the number of new elements that are introduced. The step into the neighborhood community introduces a new center of security with new adults and new contemporaries, a new neighborhood. At about the same time, his world includes a church school with other new adults and still other new contemporaries. This new world requires new independence, so even the home becomes different. His home permits more freedom to visit friends, to play on the playground, to go to the store, but also assigns more responsibility, like handling an allowance, cleaning his room, keeping track of his property, or caring for pets. Before middle childhood is over, music lessons, dancing lessons, junior choir, Cub Scouts, father-son Y-Indian Guides, and camping may enter this world.

One of the high lights of this world of middle childhood is his aquaintance with men—especially his father. While many fathers spend time with their sons before this period, the boy is never so eager to have the companionship of Dad as at this stage. In fact, he has been rather keen on Mother during the last few years. Some students of childhood refer to the period of three to five years as the family romance. Some child experts believe these are the days when the son is "in love" with his mother. He is going to marry her and is sometimes jealous of her love for his father. By middle childhood, however, he has discovered that he cannot have her for himself and that if he does want someone like her, he will have to become like Dad. Father becomes the man of all wisdom and competence, his son's hero. He glories in Dad's power and companionship. Boys are eager for his company and Dad had better get acquainted with him now. Dad cannot postpone it, for these days do not come again. If taken now, they can become the basis for enduring understanding.

Developmental tasks of middle childhood

In middle childhood, the tasks needing most attention, or the ones most crucial if the boy is to move ahead eagerly, are those that prepare him for this new world into which he is moving. As in earlier sections, the major tasks have an asterisk (*) before the numeral.

*1. *Feeling accepted by the adult person or persons in his intimate world who exemplify the ideal way of acting to him.*

In a sense this is not a developmental task, for it is not a direct achievement of the boy. It is a feeling about himself, a self-image that he can respect. Since, however, this acceptance is essential to healthy achievement of the other tasks and is related to his acceptance of adult values, it is listed as a developmental task.

In middle childhood, the persons whom the boy idealizes and from whom he seeks acceptance are most likely to be his teacher and his father. It might also include a club leader later in middle childhood, but this is not so important as the teacher and his father. If the club leader does not accept him, he can drop out of the club, but he cannot drop out of either his family or his school. His mother might possibly substitute for his father for a time, but at the loss of his developing a clear picture of his masculine role. Where there is no father, a male relative, neighbor, club leader, or some other man is important in playing this role. Dad, however, is the ideal person. If the boy does not feel accepted by his teacher, he will find it next to impossible to respond to the school expectancies placed upon him.

Unfortunately, both of these persons are beyond his command. His success in moving ahead depends on the attitude of others toward him and the actual communication of their attitude to him through word and action. However, the boy is not as helpless as may seem, for if he has found his world trustworthy as a baby, he has developed a pattern of accepting the behavior which the adults close to him have expected of him. He will approach other adults with this pattern of acceptance of adult behavior and an eagerness to please them. In doing so, he tends to draw from them the acceptance he needs so much to have.

*2. *Having ability to share affection.* The boy in middle childhood should be developing ability to share the affection of his family and his friends. This must grow naturally. It cannot be forced. He cannot "put on an act" as adults often do. He must find it pleasant to have others around; then he will be ready to show friendliness and include them in the group. If he feels confident in his parents' love and knows he does not have to fight for their approval or recognition, he will find it easy to feel kindly toward others. Sharing grows out of fellow feeling.

Ability to share his parents with his brothers and sisters is often a difficult step. It is easier to share the affection of those he loves with people who are not around so often. Family sharing grows out of the feeling that all are equal and important in family love. No one has a special place. Helping children plan for the arrival of each new baby will keep them inside the family circle and will minimize the feeling that they are being superseded.

Children should have chances to share in family surprises for one another. They should have happy experiences in giving and receiving family gifts. They can show sympathy when someone is hurt. They can learn that others have feelings and wishes, too. They can learn to be gentle with babies and pets. This is a wonderful age for a boy to have a pet. It gives him exercise in love and a feeling of being needed and appreciated every day.

Maintaining total family activity together, being sure that each has a share, will develop family solidarity. This will also provide opportunities for the teaching of group games, for learning to take one's turn, and for understanding the importance of rules in a game.

*3. *Reaching toward independence.* The boy in middle childhood should be experimenting at independence with confidence. He should not feel that these attempts at independence endanger his position with his parents. He needs to be loved—to be wanted at home. Regardless of the attention he gets, he wants to be assured that he is loved.

The boy at this age needs opportunities to work with his mother or dad. He can share responsibility in household tasks, such as emptying baskets, clearing table, wiping dishes, putting out milk bottles. He craves praise and recognition for his performance. He needs to speak out at times while others listen. He needs the experience of sharing planning for special family occasions, holidays, picnics. Participating in the planning of family fun gives him ownership as well as experience in working with others. He will enjoy leading as well as following if parental support is near.

An allowance for an eight-year-old is a great aid to a feeling of independence. He is learning about money in school. Having some to spend gives him a sense of power and freedom; he will use it quickly for trading picture cards, for toys, ice cream or candy, but it is his. A daily allowance may be best at the start.

The boy at this age may seem to rebel at routine, but it gives him security. There should be a kindly firmness where No means No and though sparingly used, cannot be changed by tantrums or tears. When adults ask him to do things, they should explain why. Wise parents seldom find it necessary to command.

*4. *Enjoying play with a friend.* The boy in middle childhood should have ability to enjoy play and companionship with one or several friends. Parents cannot provide this companionship. A boy wants friends of his own choosing; these friends must be of his own age. Within this group there is often a special friend whom he finds exceedingly hard to share unless he feels that his friend likes him best. Wise parents will not only welcome this interest, they will encourage his play with other children of his own age. It is a sign to them that their son is growing up socially. They will want to work with him and his group, for the attitudes of these friends will have a far-reaching influence on his life.

Of course there will be quarrels and fights. He finds it hard to be called a "fraidy cat" or a "sissy." He wants admiration, not derision. The fights he has are a part of learning to play together, and parents should not be drawn into them unless someone is in danger of being hurt physically.

Leadership begins to develop in these groups but it does not remain in the same person. It shifts from one person to another. Parents must be especially careful not to insert blocks into this social development, such as insisting that he play only with certain children. A boy will have more value to others and become more acceptable to groups as he develops special abilities or skills. This is an effective place for parents to help.

*5. *Identifying with a masculine role.* The boy in middle childhood knows that girls are different from boys, and he will have discovered that our culture treats them differently and expects different things from them. This comes at an age when he is still perfectly willing to play with girls, and some of these cultural expectancies seem to have little reason as far as he can see.

He will be curious and a little anxious about sex. There is some exploration and considerable talking about sex with others of his age. Boys often compare their bodies with others. If he is made to feel physically inferior, he may begin to withdraw and to worry. His sex curiosity produces shock words, off-color jokes, giggling, laughter, and hush-hush conversation. Parents will want to answer all questions briefly but as well as they can. They should be careful not to say or do anything which will give the idea that sex is dirty. How he feels about sex at this age will depend largely upon his parents' attitude toward it.

During all this, the boy needs to be getting some clear picture of what will be expected of him as a boy instead of a girl and should be happy to accept these masculine patterns as worthy for himself. This is important and it occurs early if his life has been happy, for these are days that he turns naturally toward his father. He needs a clear picture of the masculine role and he needs it in action as well as in words. He will need some activity and companionship with older boys and men. At this age, companionship and affectionate guidance from his father are especially valuable. His relationship to men throughout life is profoundly influenced by the fellowship or friction between himself and his father at this time.

*6. *Developing finer muscle control and motor abilities.* The boy in middle childhood needs to develop large-muscle control, especially in trunk, legs, and arms. He will need vigorous activities involving running, throwing, jumping, climbing, hanging, rolling, and dodging; most of these will be developed in games and active play. This is the foundation upon which the most effective co-ordination of the smaller muscles of the hands and feet develop.

He will also want many developmental activities for small muscles, and by the end of the period he should be able to catch, bat, bounce, throw at an object, skip, pound, rake, haul, or saw. The more these are done as a part of games, the more interesting they will be. He will enjoy rhythmic activities and games. This is a good age to let him invent games.

Some of this play will be alone but some of it should be in small groups. He will still enjoy individual success more than group achievement. He will develop faster if someone can explain the simple facts of these activities to him, such as the safe way to climb and the skillful way to bat.

*7. *Feeling successful in his efforts.* The boy in middle childhood needs to feel that success attends his efforts. He wants to feel good at something, whether it is riding a bike, drawing a picture, or doing his numbers. He needs a variety of opportunities where he may feel successful. This increases his confidence and encourages him to go ahead; these successes can be in the home, in the school, or in the neighborhood. They can be work or play.

He wants a place for himself. He feels he must succeed. Lack of success makes him feel inferior and unwanted. Tall tales often grow out of his need to succeed. He will be eager to please his teacher and to keep up with his schoolmates. Parents will want to give him warm approval for his achievements. Praise or approval will encourage him in a new activity. Blame or failure discourages him. He will be worried enough by failure, without criticism from those upon whom he depends for his security. If parents' actions or attitude support his feeling of failure, he may retreat or attack. Parents will want to follow the pattern of celebrating the boy's success rather than finding fault with his weaknesses.

8. *Doing small tasks under his own power and direction.* The boy in middle childhood needs the thrill of doing small tasks under his own power. He wants chances to act on his own. The task must be within his ability and his span of interest. It must have meaning to him. It should not be a routine task where he may need reminding, but short spot-tasks where he can try his own systems, such as picking and arranging the flowers for the table, or washing the bathroom floor. Mother and Dad could help by listing some of the things they have to do that day, including several that are just his size. They could ask if he would like to take over any of the jobs. Parents might plan some family activity with him, such as a picnic, and ask what part he would like to prepare. He will enjoy doing these tasks more if he understands why the task is being done and why it is important. This will develop more confidence than working under constant supervision. In addition to praising him for his efforts, it is helpful to call what he has done to the attention of his friends and adults whom he admires.

9. *Increasing his acquaintance with his environment.* The boy in middle childhood needs opportunities to get close to simple living, to fundamentals that he can understand, like the woods, the soil, or the water.

He needs to explore, to handle, to feel many types of materials. He is curious and wants to find out about things. Day camping, visits to the farm, elementary gardening, and the like are helpful. These provide simple adventures and constructive channels of play. None of these things need be on too intensive a scale or for too long a period. The program should be active, to offset the quieter time spent at school.

*10. *Increasing his ability to take directions from others and to direct himself in the absence of authority.* The boy in middle childhood enters a larger world and is introduced to new authority in the teacher, in the school, and in the policeman on the corner. Other adults who have authority or leadership in church or the community also enter into his life. Most of these are friendly and he will transfer acceptance of adults in a loving home to these adults in the neighborhood. He will need to be able to recognize authority and become increasingly able to respond to it.

Being in the community will mean also that there are many times when adult authority will not be near and he will need to be his own authority. With the development of conscience, he has accepted the values of his culture. He has learned that some behavior was considered wrong. He should now be developing the ability to respond to his own inner authority when this outer authority is not present.

These are closely related to the idea of God as a loving Father, whose supreme values serve as a pattern for the world. This God belongs to all mankind. He is the cause behind the world. He has the answers to birth, life, death, and infinity, which puzzle children of this age. God cares for everyone. Everyone is important to him. No one is ever beyond his care and love. The boy of this age is ready for a growing knowledge of the meaning of life according to the religious faith of the family.

Major responsibilities of adults with boys in middle childhood

The major task of adults in the life of the boy of middle childhood is to help him grow up. They need to recognize the characteristics of the period, the tasks of the boy in this period, and to relate themselves to the boy in such a way that their efforts are helpful and not a hindrance.

Middle childhood is not the easy, carefree period so commonly proclaimed by adults. It represents one of the major shifts in the life of the child—the shift from his home to the community. This period presents a series of threats and challenges to his personality that require a good bit of courage. He will have this courage if he feels the world about him is trustworthy. He has given considerable testing to this world during the last few years. If he still feels secure, and this sense of security rests upon his home and the self-image he has developed, he will undoubtedly have the foundation to master the period.

The boy of middle childhood is seeking security. Middle childhood is still the era where his moving forward depends upon the broad base of security provided by adults. This base will be necessary throughout life until he himself becomes adult, though it will not remain in such exposed prominence as now.

Despite the fact that a boy of this age is beginning to move away from being dependent upon his home, he must be sure of the love of his parents. This is the secure base upon which he will build. Without it he will be unable to grow. Most parents are entitled to unstinted praise for their work with their children in these early years that are so important in influencing the attitudes of the child for the years ahead. It is inevitable that there will be moments of tension and conflict between parent and child. These are normal occurrences in every home. It is inevitable, too, that humans will make mistakes in the most effective ways of handling some of these conflicts. These mistakes erase quickly and need cause little concern. Where love is, mistakes vanish.

Relaxed parents quickly discover during this age period that you can trust human nature. Boys themselves provide the clue to the kinds of handling they seek. They are so dependent upon family love that they tend to draw forth from the family the affection on which they thrive. Though the boy is still possessive of his parents at this stage, the parents are not possessive of the boy. He belongs to life and himself. He has a right to be himself. They want him to be himself. They will play their roles in his life in ways that permit and encourage that self to develop to its maximum. High in their priorities is to live well and completely themselves and then to live lovingly in relation to the entire family. This pattern of loving living may well be their greatest contribution to the growth of their son.

This is also a period of rapidly expanding relationships with people and new authority. Beginning school days not only means the boy's first break from home ties, but he now becomes acquainted with a new authority in his life, his teacher. He finds himself surrounded by others like himself and though he likes companions, many of them are strange to him. His individualism clashes with theirs. These companions become his rivals in winning the admiration of this new adult in their lives. At this age, when the teacher needs to know the home in order to teach and understand the child, that understanding is provided naturally, since the child's knowledge about his family goes along with him to school, and family secrets are now public.

This period of expanding relationships with children is characterized by feuding and fun. Adults should not become involved in quarrels or fights between their children and other children. Becoming involved with the parents or the children usually makes the problem worse. It is all right for a boy to fight with fists in self-defense, but it is cowardly to resort to sticks or stones. There is more honor in leaving such a scene than in engaging in fights that endanger each other physically. When a boy feels he can fight in self-defense without his parents' disapproval, he develops confidence within himself and there is less chance that he will need to fight.

Before school days began, a rather wide range of individual behavior was accepted, but now standards of performance are more commonly understood and parents want their offspring to measure up to other children. The community expects it, too. All this begins to bear down on the child and he finds it less painful to conform wherever he can. With this increased pressure on learning and performance, it is well to remember that the child's ability to learn or to perform depends more upon his feeling able to learn and upon his interest in learning than it does upon his age. Trying to push him ahead of his feelings usually results in hindering him rather than helping him. Understanding adults will not try to meet his stubborn moments with more pressure. They will recognize them as indications that a change of approach is needed.

The boy now finds himself under pressures exerted by his home, his school, his community, that he accept their culture and that he live up to their expectancies. He discovers a beginning pressure from his friends and playmates that he conform to their wishes. Where are the most strategic places for adults to help, and what can they do beyond providing security?

Adults can provide opportunities for the boy to become good at something. This is a period for instruction and encouragement as well as free play. It is the period when every boy needs elementary acquaintance with fundamentals in the activity in which he is engaging. This does not mean long, tedious lectures, but simple things like holding a bat, catching a ball, cleaning a brush, driving a nail, scraping a plate, making a kite, walking on stilts, riding a bike. These are the kinds of things taught by companionship in the day-to-day living.

Adults can provide materials appropriate for the age, such as paints, sand box, roller skates, collection albums. This does not mean going to a store and buying out the toy department. It means taking the lead from the child's interest and encouraging him to explore hobbies, games, skills.

Adults can stimulate and motivate interest in new activities. They can take trips, visit museums, go to a farm, listen to television, try fishing, watch things being made, catch frogs, pop corn, attend a fair together. Adults can provide special opportunities for special places for the boy to go to alone, like day camp, playground, museum classes, music series.

Adults can provide opportunities for special instruction, such as dancing, swimming, arts and crafts, piano, choir.

Adults can provide encouragement, praise, recognition. They can make the boy feel his efforts are good. Care must be taken that he is not under pressure. He will set his pace. Pressure may defeat the goal. He may feel he is not satisfactory. He will often enjoy these activities more if he can do them with a favorite friend.

Adults can help the boy be successful in his relationships with others. Adults can enrich the play life of a group and enlarge the adventure of an experience. They can also help the members plan some of the rules to guide their activities. They can do this with informal groups in the backyard and with well-organized groups. Adult supervision can be arranged co-operatively by neighbors or by taking advantage of community services, or by working co-operatively with some national agencies. Foremost among these national agencies with programs for boys of this age are Y-Indian Guides, where fathers introduce their son into an organized group experience and work or play right along with him for a few years, until the boy gets established and wants to move along with a group of his own. The age range covers the age of middle childhood. It is the type of program that enables the adult to contribute to all of the basic tasks of the boy in an atmosphere of high companionship and fun. Coming at an age when the boy thinks his dad is the greatest man in the world, it is especially helpful. The activity program ranges as wide as the combined imagination of father and son. This is an unusually rich combination. The more common activities include group games, camping, swimming, boating, fishing, singing, Indian dancing, storytelling, crafts, hobbies, scrapbooks, talks with the Great Spirit, Indian lore, picnics, cookouts, nature lore, parties, socials, and trips. Cub Scouting is another national program serving the boy in middle childhood, beginning at age eight, with a rich, proven program. In all group activities with boys of this age, the leadership should focus on the individual boy.

The leader is working with boys in a group rather than with a group of boys.

Adults can help boys in middle childhood in their reaching toward independence. Families have rich opportunities in encouraging boys of this age to share in planning family experiences, to make choices, or to help make rules through open discussions around the dinner table. Toward the end of this age, the family council can be very effective, but it is not usually introduced until some child in the family is about eight years old. Formal sessions are not necessary at this age. The main need is an opportunity to plan and to make choices. Adults outside the family can follow the same principle of giving boys opportunities to plan and to make choices as a means of helping them establish confidence in their ability to handle life.

Another rich opportunity for the family to encourage independence is through the providing of an allowance. Training in the handling of money comes through the handling of money and this is a responsibility carried primarily by the home. An increase in the allowance can be related to his acceptance of increased responsibility around the home. The boy at this age likes to be paid for chores done around the house. This gives him evidence of his independence—which is of more value to him than the money received. Praise should be generous, but it should be for specific acts and in terms he can understand.

Adults in the community can help boys establish a clear picture of their masculine role. While this is primarily an outgrowth of his relationship to his father, neighborhoods and communities could be much more friendly to boys of this age than they often are. Communities have all kinds of weeks from "Book Week" to "Be Kind to Animals Week." Maybe there ought to be a week of being friendly to children. Too many boys of this age are unknown or unspoken to (except in receiving orders) in the average community. Once a boy starts to school he should be receiving the friendly greetings of the men in the community whether they know his name or not. What becomes of the boys of the community is everyone's concern.

If all of us would remember that these boys in middle childhood are meeting mighty big tasks and that they are eagerly trying to grow up within the pattern of their own nature, the wishes of their parents, and the demands of their culture with the limited experience they have, we would admire their efforts more often than we do. More important, we would become relaxed and patient, and hopefully we would be able to enjoy living with our children.

CHAPTER 14

How a Boy Develops in Late Childhood (Ages 9-10-11)

Prelude

A boy is nature's answer to the false belief that there is no such thing as perpetual motion. In late childhood he seems to have a million muscles to keep him busy and all of them are active. Teachers grow gray trying to keep him quiet, and mothers never catch up with the holes he puts in his clothing. He has been described as one who can "swim like a fish, run like a deer, balk like a mule, bellow like a bull, act like a pig, or carry on like a jackass, according to climatic conditions."

The world of late childhood

The world of late childhood is distinguished not by the change in the number of elements but by the shift in relationships among these elements. His world is still pretty much the world of middle childhood. He is still a part of the same family, attends the elementary school of middle childhood, lives in the same neighborhood, meets pretty much the same friends, goes to the same church. His area of travel may be a little larger, his special skills and opportunities for skill instruction have probably increased, and his responsibilities around home have become larger and more important. In all respects it appears to be just a little more of what was going on in middle childhood, if one looks at the surface. But it is a vastly different world and the difference is in the new relationships that are being established between the people in it.

Up to late childhood the boy lived in a world dominated by adults and adult authority. He identified with them and accepted their values. He depended upon them for his sense of security. This was the base from which he was able to go forward in his loving and his learning. He was even possessive of the adults around him because they were so necessary to his security. In middle childhood boys and girls played together. Though they were increasingly conscious of different cultural expectancies, this did not affect their play. Now everything is shifting, not just a little, but turning practically upside down. Of course it does not occur overnight or on any particular day, but the years of late childhood are the years of great shift.

When this shift of late childhood ends, there will be a new central need in a boy's life and it will be located in a new group. Throughout infancy and childhood his central need had been security and it centered in his home, his parents and other adults like them, such as his teacher, his group leader, adult family friends who liked him and believed in him. He loves his parents, yet resents their interference with his activities; some rebellion against authority occurs. He will accuse parents of not understanding him; but there are times when he reveals his need for their comfort, confidence, security.

Now his central need is adequacy and it centers in a group of his own age and sex, in a group of his peers, in his own neighborhood and school. More than this, it centers in a group where the other members are much like himself. He chooses an alliance where he will feel adequate, where there will not be too much competition. Within this group he will respond to group codes and be loyal to all their secrets. He will idealize the group's leader (his peer), often the one best skilled in games or most daring in opposing adult standards and regulations. He must; how else can he be secure? Fortunately he can still run back to his parents if life in the group becomes too threatening, but this will be only for a time. Sometimes he turns to an adult outside his family for help, a leader or teacher admired for his skills. Understanding adults will appreciate the importance and the difficulty of this shift and be patient with his efforts. It is his biggest step toward independence and emancipation. It is a necessary step toward growing up. It is difficult because it is accompanied by some sense of insecurity and anxiety, sometimes even guilt. He becomes increasingly sensitive to wrongdoing as his conscience grows. He makes fewer demands upon his parents' time. He is busy with his own activities and friends. Mother need not be home when he returns from school, but he still needs to know when to expect her. Father is not demanded as formerly; but the boy likes discussions with him. Family trips are still enjoyed.

He is afraid of failing, of not being as good as those about him, of being a sissy. He is anxious about his body. He is often self-conscious about undressing in his mother's presence. He will be embarrassed by his parents' open display of affection, and will reject romance in movies or plays as being "mushy."

Despite his anxieties, he is beginning to feel self-sufficient, relaxed and casual.

Parents who feel this shift taking place should view it with pride, despite its difficulties. Their son is moving forward toward manhood. He is now seeking to overcome some of the small-child dependence on his parents. It is a sign they have played their role in the life of the boy so well that he feels able to test stepping out on his own. When this shift is completed in early adolescence, productive relationships between a boy and his family take on a new pattern.

Developmental tasks of late childhood

In late childhood the tasks needing most attention, or the ones most crucial if the boy is to move ahead eagerly in an orderly development of personality, are related to this shift from the home and adult center for security to his own age and sex contemporaries for security and effectiveness.

It is a much smaller list than that for middle childhood; but all of these tasks represent achievements on his part. Many of those of early childhood depended in large part upon his relationship with his home. All developmental tasks are listed below and those needing major attention have an asterisk (*) before the numeral.

*1. *Feeling accepted and effective as a member of his own age and sex contemporaries.* This feeling about himself is again related to the kind of a self-image that he can respect. It builds upon the image he has of himself as being able to become a man and upon his feeling that he is good at something. The foundation, of course, is the security he feels, but he is not conscious of this now. Later, in adolescence, he will want a feeling of a new kind of adequacy. Right now he will settle for a little less. He needs only to be able to contribute enough so he can hold a place in the group. To feel adequate would be wonderful to him, but these are days when he is just beginning to step into group life. He is testing his ability to become a part of the group. He has one foot in the group and one foot on the sure security of his home and friendly adults. He shifts his weight to the group slowly, as one tests his weight in a boat. If it will sustain him, he will gain the confidence he needs and place both feet in the boat. If the boat rocks too much, he can shift back to the adult security where he is sure. Now in late childhood he can shift back and forth. This is the pattern of growth, two steps forward and one backward, but he is inching forward.

2. *Beginning to find joy in making others happy.* The boy in late childhood needs to experience the thrill of making

others happy through what he has shared, or through what he has been able to contribute. Up to this time he has been thinking mostly of himself. Of course he has been trying to please adults, but this is largely because they will praise him. This is the period when some of the admiration he had reserved for himself and adults near him can be extended to include others. It is natural that this sometimes includes rather new friendly adults. The boy is expressing a feeling toward these adults which he has toward his parents but finds hard to express to them because they represent an authority and a protection from which he is trying to be free. This does not mean that he should not center a good deal of attention upon himself. It is more—doing unto others what he wants them to do to him and occasionally even making them happy at some cost to himself. In late childhood he needs the thrill that comes from making others happy, without necessarily any conscious return to himself at the moment. It is the beginning of a nonpossessive love upon which a happy relationship with others depends.

*3. *Responding to the group, yet feeling he can rely on his home.* The boy in late childhood wants to please the group but he also wants to please adults. During this period the balance swings slowly, sometimes imperceptibly, from the adults to the group. It is the move from the childhood dependence on parents toward independence. For a time he will replace his dependence on parents with a dependence on the group. Right now he wants to respond to the tug of the group without losing the feeling that he has the support of his parents. This is why they should support him in the group but also keep him a good member of the family. He likes to be included in the family plans as often as possible. He is ready for creative participation in a family council or some other conference plan.

This is a time when parents can keep him as a good member of the family and help him move toward independence at the same time. They can plan together regarding those rules that seem necessary for happy family living. These decisions need no longer be the sole responsibility of parents. The boy's growing sense of rules and justice, gained in play, can be developed around home and family, too. Planning about bed time, piano lessons, home work, allowances, putting away personal belongings, watching TV, can be handled in an atmosphere of mutual respect, individually or in a family council. An appeal to reason will get good response when it is not being used to force him to accept some decision previously made. This planning includes responsibility as well as freedoms. It should be enlarged to involve planning for the whole family as well as just for himself.

Along with their new treatment of him as a person with ideas worth considering, he needs new privileges for adventure and privacy. He would like a room of his own if possible. In any case, he needs a home where he has some new privileges, such as a place where he can make a mess if he cleans it up, a place where he can make noise, a place where he can bring part of the gang, the privilege of having a friend in to lunch or overnight. He needs experiences in planning, in handling his own money, in making decisions, even making mistakes. He needs all this, however, within a clear pattern of family living. He needs to understand the range of freedom, especially the limits. Every boy should carry some part of the necessary routine in the home. He will enjoy special tasks of short duration where he can feel pride in their accomplishment.

*4. *Winning his way with a group.* The boy in late childhood not only needs a friend but he must be able to become a member of a group with others like himself. At nine years of age he needs a friend. By ten and eleven years of age he needs a group. All the group members need not be intimate friends, but he wants a group and needs to know that they want him. This group will be like himself not only in sex, organic development, and strength, which correlate roughly with age and grade, but also often in interests. As he steps from the adult value system to the value system of his peers, he seeks to be in a group which is most like himself. Those who differ from him are a threat to his adequacy. In communities where the environment seems threatening to him, a wider range of ages will be found in his group.

He will begin to consider himself a big fellow as quickly as he feels sure of himself in the group. It is important for a boy to learn how to give and take; this will help him learn to get on well with others. He will become loyal to their codes and passwords. He will submit without complaint to more rules than his parents ever tried to impose. Whatever the group decides will be law. It means a new development in his respect for law and authority, rules and justice, "followership" as well as leadership. To hold his place he will learn that he must be loyal, courageous, and a good sport. He is upset if he discovers the group will not accept him. In this case he may retreat to books, television, hobbies, or the like, and say he does not like the group.

*5. *Accepting his masculine role in his group life.* The boy in late childhood needs to achieve a strong identification with those of his own sex and age. Up to this period boys and girls played together, but the separation becomes marked in late childhood and the boy should be aligning himself with the fellows and tending to leave the girls to play by themselves.

He should picture himself as becoming a man, strong, brave, champion of the right, a protector of the weak. He should thrill to adventure and great deeds. He should enjoy the roughhouse and tussle in which this age participates. Being called a sissy is unbearable at this age. Being accepted by his group will give him the assurance he needs.

The boy in late childhood should learn what part sex will play in his life. He has serious thoughts about sex and himself. Proper parental guidance will have prevented any guilt feelings about sex play or sex practices which most children of this age have experienced. He needs information on sex development. He should understand outward phenomena, like seminal emissions, before they occur. These days when he can be objective in his interest are an ideal time to give him information and vocabulary for understanding the human body. Along with this information, he wants the chance for discussion of these things. He should have opportunities for books, lectures, pictures, talks with his parents, contact with experts who lead discussions in his group where his code is being formed.

*6. *Being confident of his ability to grow up.* The boy in late childhood needs to develop confidence in his ability to grow up. He is concerned about himself and is often anxious about his ability to be a man. He worries lest freckles, red hair, his body build, or eyeglasses will limit his development. This is especially true if he experiences difficulty in being accepted by a group.

He is both eager and worried about facing adult life. He fears failure or doing things wrong. Competition where he seems to stand alone tends to increase his worry. Individual comparison is hard to take. He needs opportunities to develop his skills and his self-confidence.

7. *Feeling useful to someone or something.* The boy in late childhood needs assurance that there is a place for him. He longs for responsibility. He wants to be useful or important. He wants to feel that he is as good as others and he wants others to notice it. One of the chief dangers in this period is the development of a feeling that he is inadequate.

He wants to be like an adult, yet he finds himself scurrying back to the protection of adults. He needs a chance to share in planning and carrying out his own program. He needs to be of value to other people, to share responsibility measured to his size. These are days for laying a firm basis for responsible citizenship. He is ready for his first tasks in the spirit of service.

8. *Increasing his acquaintance with the adult world.* The boy in late childhood needs increasing acquaintance with his community. He wonders what the adult world is like. He won-

ders about some of the things that he sees adults do. He is concerned about social problems that touch his friends, his school, and his community. He is ready to face great liberalizing ideals involving fair play and social justice. His critical sense of justice needs this experience. His conscience is moving up another rung on the ladder of social development.

9. *Daring to express his feeling for adventure.* The boy in late childhood needs to step outside the limits of family or school and feel contact with something bigger. He craves activity, more things to do, more things to learn. He wants opportunities to build things, to trail, to collect, to hike. He needs contacts close to nature, to feel the relatedness of things. Periods away from home not only encourage independence and adventure but make home more desirable to him. A summer camp provides an ideal place for creative guidance and understanding supervision. The informal adventuresome spirit of camping can be carried into activities as often as possible. A picnic where one can eat with one's fingers provides a little letdown in manners along with fun.

10. *Increasing his interest in fair play and justice.* The boy in late childhood should be developing skills in co-operation. He has a great interest in the use of rules and their fair application to life. Up till now, good and evil have depended upon adult values. Now he needs an opportunity to express his own ideas of right and wrong. Adults can make helpful suggestions in these discussions but the values developed should be his own. This is a good time to develop a respect for each individual, to encourage him in doing some work in the interest of others, and to become acquainted with the great, inspiring stories of his faith. He should participate regularly in religious services with his friends, for he needs the support that comes from knowing that God cares for him and does not expect the impossible. He should understand that all men are God's children, therefore of infinite worth, and that none should be exploited.

Major responsibilities of adults with boys in late childhood

The major responsibility of adults in the life of a boy in late childhood is to help him so to increase confidence in himself and in his competence in dealing with his environment that he feels able to shift from the childhood dependency on his parents toward achieving acceptance in a group of his own age and sex contemporaries.

This is not an easy task. It marks the completion of a phase of growth started in middle childhood. In those years, the big challenge was to step out from his home into the larger community. Now, in a few short years, he is expected to begin feeling so secure in this community that he is willing to surrender most of the security he has learned to count upon in his home. The wonder is that he makes the shift at all, rather than that he is often anxious about it.

This is a time for parents to encourage him in his efforts rather than to hold him back. Those who find it hard to take his mild efforts at independence in late childhood, and succeed in their efforts to possess him now, will face a much more violent time in early adolescence. Late childhood is the period for him to take these steps toward security with his peers. He can still return to the family or friendly adults if his contemporaries seem too threatening, without feeling worried about his inadequacy. This will not be so acceptable in adolescence. If he achieves this security with his contemporaries now, he will find a new companionship with adults in early adolescence.

Adults who enjoy seeing a boy grow up will find plenty of satisfaction in these years of nine, ten, and eleven. Each period in the growing up process has its thrills, but there is a special joy in late childhood. Despite the task he is facing at this age, the boy seems to be at a high level of personal character. He has an ability to live with both adults and his fellows. He presents a sort of preview of the man he will become. He seems to stand upon a plateau of achievement from which he looks forward toward adulthood for a brief time before he rushes forward into adolescence. Actually these are grand years to live with a boy—and they can grow finer year after year. Each hour of thrills is balanced by moments of anxiety, but the parent with the long view will see these upsetting moments as stages in the development of a growing personality—a personality that is living very much in the present.

It is hard to know what will cause the greatest anxiety for adults in this period. It may be the unending body activity of the boy, the noise he loves so much, the way he hangs his clothes on the floor, the names he hurls at girls, his growing independence from the home, or the authority he gives to the gang. Each in turn will have its barb, and because adults over the years have developed habits of being protective and in authority, these new developments are often disturbing. But growing boys will not stay put, and adults cannot expect that one adjustment will settle the issue. It becomes one adjustment after another. Those who want to help him grow up will want to be sure they are playing on his team with him rather than against him. It is so much easier to try to carry on the old pattern of dealing with him than to shift to the new role adults must take.

Adults can encourage the boy to move toward greater independence. He must feel free to grow and move from the home without guilt feelings if he is to find real satisfaction in being more independent. The atmosphere in which a healthy personality grows is one of love and understanding. This is a period when he is in special need of that kind of help.

The boy begins to take life into his own hands. This is quite a delicate period in the life of the child. While he is being gently encouraged to grow toward independence, he cannot be pushed aside when he rushes back to the dependent status. Talking things over together at those times when he wants to talk, or continuing reading together, even though he can read, is helpful. The families will want a routine and a consistency that will enable him to predict their reaction to his behavior. Having a routine, they should try to operate as free from rules or regulations as possible. Family living will want to be relaxed and casual, yet reasonably orderly.

Authority gives way to guidance, and adults who do not recognize the boy's need for independence may try to retreat to the days of their old authority, only to find they no longer possess it. If they resort to disciplinary measures, they will probably upset their digestion more than the boy's. Most lies are due to fear of punishment, or to avoid the grown-up's disapproval. That is a high price to pay for relying on an authoritarian approach which is doomed to failure anyway. Almost all disciplinary measures occur too often with the child. Furthermore, most of them are not necessary. Adults who appreciate the boy's struggle toward independence will not find his behavior so serious. They will see opportunities for helpful, friendly guidance when he is in the mood to accept it. At other times they will smile quietly to themselves as they watch these early steps toward adult status.

Boys of this age can be helpful around the home but they will need lots of reminding. Short, understandable tasks for which they can take the responsibility and which they can do well catch their enthusiastic response. They should be able to do jobs by themselves and know that they are well done. Their own approval, supported by a pat on the back from adults, is helpful in building confidence and independence.

A family council will be enjoyed by boys of this age if they can have a real chance to share in the planning of the family work and family entertainment. A boy will not be interested in a council where he listens to decisions made some place else and reported to the council. He is ready to be taken into the family corporation as a partner, and partners speak as well as listen. A family bulletin board with calendar for recording dates, for posting jokes, for tacking notes, and for display of family achievements can become quite a center of family life and interest.

Boys of this age are still interested in having an allowance and it is important that their training in handling money be under way at this age. They should have experience in earning, spending, and giving. Saving has little value in money handling unless the boy is saving in order that he may buy something more costly than his weekly allowance permits.

Adults can help the boy develop experience with a group. Adults will want to encourage their child in his urge to find membership in some group of boys of his own age. At an age when a boy is developing fast, it is especially important that his most intimate associates be boys of his own strength and development. These are usually found in his own age group or grade. The best companionship for a boy in the fourth grade (all things being equal) is another boy in the fourth grade. The authority the boys begin to give their group may be startling, but this is a stage in their maturing. Adults who understand welcome this growing interest in friends outside the home and a boy's preference to be with those friends, even though it may upset the Sunday trip planned for the entire family.

Parents will do well to see that there are organized, purposeful groups with adult leadership in the neighborhood, even if they have to start the groups themselves. If some character-building, youth-serving agency exists in the community, its leaders will be happy to work with parents in forming these clubs. This kind of contact will enhance the boys' club life even more. The groups should remain small (from eight to twelve boys) so that the boys can have the greatest possible opportunities for planning and managing their own activities. This opportunity to make decisions and manage their own affairs is especially important, for this is the thing that makes the club desirable. Parents can enrich the group life by having some of the dads plan with the leader about once a month. These activities should usually be something greater than the boys could arrange by themselves. Action rather than watching is desirable because it is more adventuresome. As dads participate in the club life, the boys get to know other men intimately. These men are in a strategic position to reveal the values by which they guide their lives. This can be done naturally around a campfire or along the trail. The boys may not say much but they will drink it in. They want to become adult.

The boy in late childhood likes football, baseball, bowling, skating, fishing, swimming, camping, trailing, shooting, or hiking. He enjoys trips to interesting places like historic spots, airports, scientific museums, athletic events, amusement parks, a circus, or a television broadcast. He likes to question interesting people who bring things they can see and handle—the explorer, scientist, athlete, hunter, hobbyist, traveler. His interest is high in science and inventions, prehistoric animals, astronomy and possible life on other worlds, personalities, discoveries. Collecting still continues. Dramatic play is still exciting. He enjoys roughhousing; friendship with boys is partly expressed by pushing, tumbling, wrestling. These interests can be incorporated into the group's program.

Adults can provide opportunities for the boy to develop special skills and abilities. The boy in late childhood has developed enough small-muscle co-ordination to become quite skillful in many activities that are respected by a group. These will make him of more value to the group. He has also developed ability to take training and coaching for short periods, which he then can put into practice through endless hours of play. Many of the athletic fundamentals are learned quickly at this stage; and opportunities to have coaching in running, throwing, jumping, softball, tumbling, tennis, swimming, wrestling, and elementary team play will add to his joy and confidence throughout life. Athletics that stress co-operative play should be included as well as those that stress individual development.

In middle childhood the goal of such teaching was not the development of skill as much as an acquaintance with the enjoyment of an activity; while this still ranks high as a goal in late childhood, the development of skill is often amazing.

This is still the age of making things and a boy will enjoy the use of tools, handcrafts, and simple machines, especially if they make noise. He will want to take things apart and put them together, try new combinations, even harness the neighbor's cat. Adults can provide places and tools that can be used for this kind of adventuring and skill training (minus the cat).

The care of pets and the raising of their young requires many skills that the boy in late childhood can master. Some even develop great competence in speaking about, or demonstrating with their pets.

The creative and entertaining skills are usually started in this period. Boys become quite creative in art mediums, adept in magic, or skillful in some musical instrument. Late childhood is the time to explore until he finds some skills that catch his interest and challenge his ability. Adults can provide these opportunities and the encouragement to participate in them. Participation will usually be in the company of a friend.

Adults can help the boy increase his confidence in his ability to grow up. Success is very important to the boy in late childhood. It is always important, but especially at this age, because he is trying to shift his base of security and any success makes this easier.

Success in school is very important. He wants success to keep up in the eyes of his mates. Adults want him to succeed and are often concerned that he keep up in the eyes of the neighbors. Comparisons of his performance with that of others is hard on him and does not develop a healthful outlook on life. Repetition of a grade in school should have occurred, if at all, in the first three grades, rather than now.

The boy must be given freedom to develop his own ideals, interests, aptitudes, and abilities. It is especially important that he should not be tortured by ideals fixed too high, or blocked by vocational expectancies that parents have set up in their minds for him. Success comes to the boy who feels able and ready to go ahead. Criticism and nagging only handicap him. Adults who really want to help should be helping him develop confidence in himself.

Adults can help the boy to enjoy his masculine role and to express it in play and activities with those of his own sex. This is still an age when he needs a clear picture of the masculine role, and he needs to see it in action in his own home and in the neighborhood. Contact with many friendly adult men in the neighborhood is desirable. These adults can work or play along with the boys in their group activities and their games. Men are not only important to the world's work but they can do things together that are fun—which is the key to accepting this role with enthusiasm.

Parents who feel anxious or insecure about answering sex questions will get few questions from now on. Most children learned the story of human birth before this time and they have discovered whether or not the family is an available and a reliable source of information. Those who still have the child's confidence will give short, accurate answers and treat the subject naturally. Punishment for acts growing out of curiosity or exploration only tends to make the problem greater by fixing it in the boy's emotions.

The big task for adults with boys in late childhood is to shift the child's life into his own hands as he shows willingness to grasp it. It is a period for encouraging rather than pushing. It is a period for shifting from authority to guidance. It is a period demanding more tolerance for noise, activity, messes, arguments, and secretiveness. Pre-eminently it is a period for adults to maintain a balanced view of life themselves, sticking to fundamentals but quite often blind to the lesser mistakes of late childhood. Easy does it.

CHAPTER 15

How a Boy Develops in Early Adolescence (Ages 12-13-14)

Prelude

The zest with which the early adolescent does an errand is equalled only by the speed of a turtle on a July day. This boy can do the chores around his home with three or four adults to prod him, though he can do similar chores all day at a friend's house and enjoy them. *But* a man is being born. Arms and legs are defying sleeves and pants to keep up with them. Favorite adults are being imitated. Even his hair renews its acquaintance with the comb and the pomade when some cute new girl moves into the next block.

The world of early adolescence

The world of the early adolescent is bewildering, filled with strong and conflicting pressures. The intensity of that conflict, its storm and stress, will be conditioned by the opportunity the boy has had to achieve a feeling of independence prior to the arrival of puberty.

In late childhood, he was experimenting with the transfer

of his security from his home to a group of his contemporaries. He felt ready for that transfer, but now, when his security seems tenuous in both places, he is hit by an avalanche. He is hit so hard, in fact, that some of early childhood's struggles of independence and negativism need to be fought all over again.

In struggling to become himself, to establish the self-image he can respect, to become self-sufficient, he may seem to reject his parents. Their authority and their very existence as adults are perpetual reminders that he is not yet an adult though he feels more adult. Toward his parents and other adults he becomes more secretive and resists being pressured for explanations. Parental love is still deeply necessary to give him security; though he depends upon it, he will seldom acknowledge it—even disclaiming any signs of his need for that love.

In searching for the kind of person he can be, he discovers that both the community and his parents are constantly demanding a new competence from him. He sees that he is being judged by outsiders solely on his own performance rather than that of his family. Actually he wants to merit the respect of his parents and other adults, but he is not certain that he does. He is often unsure about what those who are judging him really expect of him. So he feels that they judge him unfairly and fail to understand him. Never has he worried so much about what is the right thing for him to do. As a result of this and his new sex role, he is often self-conscious.

This is a period, too, of high idealism despite a growing indifference to formal religion. He has gained in his ability to do abstract thinking. He enjoys debates about personal subjects or problems and about the new values he is setting for himself. He becomes highly critical of his family's shortcomings, particularly their failure to meet any of his new standards.

There is a growing awareness of the conflicts between his parents' standards and those of his group, to which he turns even more desperately for anchorage. The group's authority supplants his family's, and he resents having his friends chosen for him. Approval by his friends and conformity to group standards take on new importance. The other members of his group are subject to the same conflicts as he is, so they demand great conformity for mutual self-defense against the adult world. This explains why some of these relationships become so intense at times, both in affection and in rivalry that is sometimes violent, as in teen "gang wars." Ability to lead reveals itself strongly and grows rapidly in this atmosphere. There is a rising consciousness of differences between his group and other groups. This may express itself in racial or intercultural intolerance unless a bedrock foundation of democratic thinking has been established.

Not only the forces outside him but internal forces as well have thrust him forward into this world of confusion. With the rapid development of his reproductive organs and secondary sex characteristics came radically new feelings for which he could not be fully prepared. According to the stage of this physical maturation, he shows increasing interest in the female sex which he had considered worthless. He may first show this interest by taunting and teasing them, as though to defend himself against the strong propulsion he has toward them and against the emotional stirrings they inspire. Soon there will be co-ed parties, "gang dates," and solo performances. He is interested in gaining social skills that will reduce his discomfort in the presence of girls and his sensitivity to ridicule by them or in front of them. He may be further confused by the greater maturity of girls of his own age, emphasizing even more his feeling that he is not approaching adulthood fast enough. His new attitude toward the opposite sex sometimes extends to his mother, and he responds to her as a feminine personality, treating her with a show of gentility.

His new physical development in size and strength increases his capacity for enjoyment of athletics and outdoor activities. He takes great pride in excelling in any of them. With his increased enthusiasm, he tends to overdo in sports. His vigor and enthusiasm combine with his need for group activities with his contemporaries to throw him excitedly into the often strenuous rivalry of team sports. Parallel with this, his interest in individually conducted hobbies wanes unless he can transfer such interests to the group sphere, as in camera clubs. Science, invention, and mechanics (primarily as "masculine" interests) and history and travel (especially as they satisfy his craving for action, excitement, and adventure) are now even more important than before. He is less interested in making things unless they are related to his group activities. Though he is now reaching the height of his unenthusiasm for work around his home, he is eager to earn money, which so insistently symbolizes maturity. He may spend the money he earns in treating the friends in his gang in group activities, on girls or on clothing that he feels impresses them; or he may hoard it to buy the automobile he'll drive when he's old enough to get his license; or he may save for his college education, toward which his entrance into junior high or high school has brought him one step closer.

Developmental tasks of early adolescence

In early adolescence the tasks needing most attention, or the ones most crucial if the boy is to move ahead eagerly in an orderly development of personality, deal with the boy's readjustment to his topsy-turvy world. They comprise a formidable list of achievements for these three short years. Their coming at a time when his confidence in those most interested in him is at a low point makes these tasks even more difficult.

In these cross-sectional studies, the most important tasks have an asterisk (*) before the numeral. All the tasks in this section are considered major tasks.

*1. *Feeling wanted by his contemporaries and feeling able to contribute to them.* The boy who has developed a core of self-acceptance in childhood can build upon that in these upset days. Any sense of security will make him more attractive in a world characterized by insecurity. These are days when competence in athletic or artistic skills will be a great support. For a time they can compensate for lack of social skills. He will be sought because of the competence his skills give to the group. Until this feeling of adequacy is developed, the boy will be forced to center his attention upon himself.

*2. *Developing an acquaintance with and some at-homeness with girls: feeling worthy of love.* The boy now normally seeks the attention and interest of the opposite sex. This may come early or late—but when it does, success is very important to him. In the beginning, success is achieved if he is seen with an attractive or popular girl by his associates. Group life provides an easy approach to dating, which is likely to be in doubles or groups. Most boys need information about what girls expect of them. They want to know how to ask for a date, what to do on a date, how to be interesting to the girl, how much to spend, what to do about a good-night kiss, and what a girl expects in manners. As long as girls baffle him, a boy will not move easily toward activities with them. As he matures, his interest grows beyond how much prestige dating brings to him. He discovers the joys of companionship and the thrill of making a girl happy. This is when he begins to feel worthy of love.

*3. *Being eager and increasingly able to direct his own life within reasonable tension.* The boy now wants a chance to direct his own life independently. It is hard to feel free unless one knows from what one is trying to free oneself. So he finds himself struggling for independence from his family and recognition by his group. Inevitably he is involved in a conflict between his family and his group, and he must resolve it without feeling guilty. Once he feels sure that he is competent to direct his own life, he becomes conservative and tends to return to the great attributes he developed in childhood.

*4. *Winning and holding membership in an intimate group of his own age and sex.* The boy in early adolescence needs the companionship and approval of his associates. He must have intimate relationships with someone while he is struggling to free himself from his parents; so he turns to his group. He needs to be sure that he really belongs, that he can count on them as his friends. He sees himself through the eyes of these associates. He can stand almost any disapproval except theirs. His happiness is associated with their achievements and their recognition of him as a valuable person. The more he is able to contribute to the life of the group through his own skill, the easier it will be for him to hold membership in it. He will be unhappy and uncomfortable outside of the group. He will need to pay the price of loyalty and comformity to hold his membership.

*5. *Understanding his body and developing positive attitudes toward sex life.* The boy in early adolescence needs to understand what is happening to his body. He must have the facts about his growing up. Normal changes occurring within his body should not give him cause for concern or alarm. His understandings should carry beyond the physical facts into a growing realization of the power and dignity of his body. He needs an understanding of how sex contributes to life and to his personal fulfillment. He needs to understand what is happening to the female body as well as to his own. He needs to envision himself as becoming a man and to feel that others look upon him as a masculine person. The changes that have been occurring have been so sudden that he often wonders if he will be able to function adequately as a man. He needs opportunities to picture himself as a man and to act like a man. A sport fitted to his body structure and skill will help him gain competence and confidence in his physical activity.

*6. *Feeling confident that he is normal.* The boy in early adolescence needs to think well of himself, to feel that he is the same as those about him, to have assurance that he is able to handle life well. He is often so doubtful about his growing up that these assurances need to come time and again from those about him who believe in him. These assurances are especially needed if he is slow in developing.

To the boy in this period, his concept of self is closely related to his feeling about his physical body. It is the embodiment of his personality in all aspects. Furthermore, it is the revelation of his personality to others. His posture, his walk, his facial expressions, and his energy portray his feelings. If he has what are, or what he considers to be shortcomings or handicaps, he will be especially anxious about his adequacy. Following the standard of the crowd in dress and behavior, even slavishly, helps him feel that he is like others.

He needs opportunities to use his body in vigorous, outdoor activities like hiking and skating, along with experiences in individual and team sports. The more confidence he develops in his body, the sooner he will regain his emotional security. He needs to develop social interests beyond the family, to take trips away from home, to compare himself with his ideal and be satisfied.

*7. *Feeling of value to some group or cause.* The boy in early adolescence needs to feel that he has value to other people, that he is needed right now in some cause or group. He needs to feel a part of something bigger than himself, even though it means some personal sacrifice. Having a part in carrying forward some of the ideals of mankind makes him feel a part of the creative force of the world.

The family will hardly be able to provide opportunities that are big enough to satisfy this need. These opportunities will come from the school, the church, the community, or some organization in which he is a member. He will prefer to participate in these causes or programs as a part of a group.

*8. *Increasing his experience with the world in which he lives.* The boy in early adolescence needs firsthand acquaintance with the world in which he lives. He needs opportunities for contact with wholesome adults, opportunities to increase his range of travel and experience. He needs to see the relation of work to things produced. It is desirable that he have work opportunities to supplement his allowance. As he tries to picture his place in life, he needs to be looking for his place in the world of work. These work opportunities should be significant, worth-while tasks, requiring responsibility and dependability. They should not be placed upon his shoulders until he is willing to accept them. Then he must be responsible.

*9. *Finding joy in the active use of his body and mind.* The boy in early adolescence needs to have fun. He needs a variety and abundance of outdoor activity and play which will provide zestful action and adventure.

Many of the leisure-time activities of this period are the quiet or spectator type, such as reading newspapers and comic books, listening to the radio, watching television, or watching others in sports or public performance.

He needs more active challenge to both his body and mind, as provided in athletics, outings, picnics, trips, camping, fishing, riding, skating, and hiking. He needs a chance to plan and prepare for adventuresome experiences, including trips away from home. Though individual, creative skills are on the decrease, group planning will provide some creative opportunities.

*10. *Becoming articulate about some philosophy of life.* The boy in early adolescence needs to feel that life has meaning and that there is a role for him to play. He must be able to express some of the values by which he guides or would like to guide his life. He needs to have opportunities to learn how other boys feel. He will profit by association with high-minded adults, and by many opportunities for discussion of the problems of his world with his contemporaries. These groups should be small enough so that his thinking will be needed.

He needs acquaintance or experience with situations of social injustice. He needs to understand why the situation occurs and what would be required to relieve it. He needs to see what reflection of this injustice occurs in situations where he lives and to test his proposed solutions. He needs a chance to contribute to programs which he understands.

From this thinking about himself and social injustice, it is only a step to the brotherhood of man and the respect for all individuals. He needs to understand that all mankind is bound together; that what he seeks for his own group, he must also seek for others. If he can take this stride, he will gain a new respect for himself. He needs to understand his relationship to the universal plan, including the universal Fatherhood of God, and to gain an understanding of prayer as a source of power which he can tap at any time.

Major responsibilities of adults with boys in early adolescence

Parents of boys who are entering into adolescence are standing on the threshold of their most thrilling or most trying period. Which of these periods it becomes for both the youth and the parent will depend more on the attitude of the parent than on the attitude of the boy. The boy's attitude is pretty well determined. He is responding to an inner demand that he become a person whom he can respect, a person able to stand on his own feet and give a good account of himself. The attitude of the parent in meeting this demand on the part of youth varies. Some attitudes lead to worry and heartaches, others to pride and joy. Here are some of the choices.

Before their child enters adolescence, some parents find it hard to believe that the close relationships that they have achieved with their child during his early years will change. When they see their son enter his teens, they may be certain that the so-called disrespect they have seen younger adolescents show toward parents will not be shown toward them. But come it will, and their disillusioned responses, such as the following, only add to the boy's confusion.

Some parents feel that the teens are something to be endured, that they must not interfere, that it will be good when it is over. Their teen-agers become confused; they feel rejected, unwanted.

Other parents respond with feelings of hurt. They say, "Look how he treats me after all I have done for him." This infantile response from adults also bewilders teen-agers. They do not have a clear, adult pattern. They become plagued by guilty feelings.

Still other parents insist that this cannot happen in their family. They put their foot down. They are going to show who is boss. Actually, they are only retreating to the pattern they used years before; but now, instead of submission, it only promotes defiance and greater difficulties.

Parents who co-operate with the adolescent are going to enjoy the supreme thrill of watching a child become a young adult. The dreams they have cherished in their hearts are about to be revealed in this personality they have prepared for its unfolding. It is as awesome a time as the moment before a painting is unveiled. The artist does not stand back and throw mud upon this masterpiece. Rather he places a deft stroke here, an admiring glance there, a loving touch to enhance his creation. Parents have been nurturing a life across the years that will step out onto the stage toward adulthood, on its own. Nothing can keep youth backstage. It is inconceivable that those who are supposed to help him should try to trip him at his entrance. In reality, it is far more thrilling than a painting or stage entrance, for this creation reveals itself slowly. Instead of being a creation by others, this new person has taken possession of himself across the months and the years, and has become self-creative.

Adults who will be helpful must understand the trying period of life in which the boy in early adolescence finds himself and must understand what he is trying to do. This is not always easy because his pattern is not always clear. Basically, he is striving for a new sense of identity as a person, a sense of identity where he sees himself as one among his fellows, sought and accepted. He must achieve this new identity on his own, apart from his family, competent to contribute to his group and the greater community. He is seeking this identity in a period when basic physiological changes and feelings have so engulfed him that most of his energy is demanded by his own struggles, and as a result he appears to be self-centered. He needs the help of adults, but they cannot do their work as directly as they could in the earlier stages of his life.

Adults can help boys win with a group. This is the adults' major responsibility in the boy's early adolescence—to help him win and hold membership in a group of his contemporaries and to support him in his efforts to contribute to the group. Success in his group membership becomes his key to developing independence, to gaining freedom from family restraints and decision-making for him, to developing acquaintance with girls, to understanding his sex role, to exploration of his world, and to more articulate expression of his philosophy of life.

Opportunities provided by the group include:

Satisfying some basic personal needs

Security—being accepted, understood, and wanted
Achievement—power to perform, to accomplish
Recognition—having worth and value to others
Adventure—desire for new experience, thrills
Friendship—intimate belonging and fellowship

Satisfying some needs for growth

Creative use of leisure hours
Training in democratic practices
Opportunities to plan and carry out projects
Co-operative adventures with his peers
Increasing responsibility for their own affairs
Expanding interests and widening the horizon
Appreciation of one's body and its fitness
Facing the conflicts of their own age

Contacts with friendly, interested adults
Acquaintance with enduring values
Deep fellowship which shares hopes and ideals
Increasing independence from parents but with affection

Satisfying some needs for community living

Growing respect for rights and privileges of others
Understanding of the social tensions
Membership in the whole human family
Growth in unselfish service
Sharing in causes that make a difference
Participation in the ideals of the race

If the boy has already participated in group activities during late childhood, this period will be much easier for both him and his parents. Parents should assess community resources for the group life their boy needs. He should be encouraged—but not pressed—to join a group or to help organize a group of boys his own age. To try to prevent his joining or forming a group is to try to block one of his greatest needs. It inevitably ends in a defeat for the parents or a permanent crippling of his adult personality. The wiser parents try to get acquainted and on good terms with the boys in their son's group, and to help them achieve the goals they've set. The wiser parents also offer help to their son if the boy accepts responsibility for any group activity.

For parents, this is a period calling for statesmanship and diplomacy. Guidance must be exerted with a delicate touch. Parents should sincerely express the feeling that they are there to be of service when needed. To interfere—or to give the impression of interference—is the sure way to bring the group's standards into conflict with adults! The surest way to help boys approach adult values is to give them reasonable freedom and to co-operate with them.

Adults can co-operate with the boys in their group life. Although the boy in early adolescence often resents having adults prying into his activity, parents have discovered that they can enrich the group life for these boys, with great profit to the group and to themselves. If co-operation is started at this early stage with a helpful, understanding attitude, it can add to the group prestige without endangering the independence of the group. Many parents have been able to continue this relationship through middle adolescence. Those who have participated in this kind of program testify that:

It builds stronger family relationships
It makes better parents
It enables parents to retain significant contact and influence with their son
It makes possible co-operative planning for youth in a community
It provides a basis for development of standards of behavior and control
It enables parents to become acquainted with their son's friends and their parents
It enables parents to keep their sons closer to home
It makes happier, more relaxed parents
It provides team work in dealing with their son
It becomes one of their greatest pleasures
It multiplies adult contacts for their son

Parents are aware that there is much they can contribute to the life of their son, but they usually find their efforts blocked or ignored. They have found that the most effective way of continuing to influence their son's attitudes and ideals is not individually with their own son, but in co-operation with other parents and their sons. It is a group of adults co-operating with a group of boys. There are great values in this collective voice for both the boys and the parents, as it conceals the individual struggles that have undoubtedly begun to develop within each family. The boys see the parents as a power to help them establish themselves as a group with prestige and power. They also discover that they are free to accept or reject this adult power. Having this freedom to reject it if they wish, they find wonderful ways of working together.

Effective planning at this level almost requires someone to negotiate between the group of parents or adults and the group of boys (though occasional suggestions by individuals might be picked up). The parents usually make plans in the light of the group needs and the resources of the parents. These are presented to the group as invitations which the boys may accept, reject, or negotiate. Parents (usually only fathers) enter into the group program individually or in twos, occasionally as a group. Typical activities by parents are:

> A club meeting every four to six weeks at a home, with the program arranged by a father and his son, or another adult. Generous but simple refreshments should be a part of this meeting.
>
> An invitation to a sports event or contest among dads and sons (fathers usually pair with some boy other than their own), such as bowling, softball, or fishing.
>
> An invitation to meet some outstanding personality known by one of the fathers and to interview this personality in this father's home.
>
> An offer to the club program chairman to provide a club surprise program if the club would set the date far enough in advance.

Once this kind of invitation pattern is initiated, the group usually responds by inviting participation in their activities. Parents who want to continue this relationship will find it advisable to participate. Typical invitations include:

> Entertainment and fellowship, such as attending dramatic performances or attending a father-and-son dinner.

Athletics, such as watching an athletic contest or a challenge to a match of some kind.

Educational programs such as parent-youth clinics, speaking to the group, judging at an arbitration council, or demonstration of a family council.

Social activities, such as being guests at a party or attending a club ceremonial.

Services of some sort, such as preparing food for a group supper, providing transportation for a trip, officiating at an athletic event, coaching in athletics or dramatics, making a costume for a play, chaperoning a party, supporting money-raising projects, or providing equipment needed by the group.

Adults can encourage and support the boy's efforts to be independent. The positive attitude toward early adolescence keeps its goal centered on the growing process. Adults help him most when they encourage him to grow. Becoming independent relies upon a core of self-acceptance. When a boy feels able to stand on his own feet, he will be emotionally liberated from his family. This sounds so simple, yet the struggle often takes so long.

Adults must expect much of the struggle and accusations to be directed against them. Often where the family ties have been the closest, the struggle will be the most severe. He rebels to prove his independence. Though it is directed toward those around him, it really reveals his inner insecurity. Rebellion is only a part of the struggle, however; it will continue until he feels competent to deal with life himself.

To oppose the struggle, therefore, and expect life to be smoothed by the exertion of more authority only accentuates the problem. Adults do not lose respect because the boy talks back, uses vile language, or attacks family codes. Adults lose respect when they act in the same way as the boy. Rebellion and unruliness will continue as long as his inner distress with his dependency and inadequacy continues. Rebellion can be reduced by avoiding emotional displays on the part of the adults, and by increasing the opportunities for the boy to attain self-respect and competence.

When someone in authority tries to talk the adolescent into some sense, it is like walking on quicksand. The best arguments sink below the surface of their own weight. The boy is not fighting ideas. He is fighting his inner incompetence. It must be taken for granted that he will make some mistakes as he searches for freedom. Adults who seem understanding will be able to give guidance. Censure is useless.

These are days to treat the boy as more grown-up, to express belief in his ability to think and act intelligently. It is a time to stretch the family rules or not try to see everything that occurs. It is a time to oppose certain kinds of behavior, but never the individual. Basically, he wants desperately to be poised and adult. He can become that most quickly if those around him include him in the planning and listen to his ideas. In fact, most adults will be impressed with how good his ideas really are.

Nine out of ten of these adolescents at a recent conference voted in favor of a family council. This conference included only several hundred, but the proportion so voting is always high. Many successful family councils include the management of the family budget. Responsible participation is the quickest path to self-respect and independence.

The early adolescent needs freedom to dress and act like the gang. Adults may not like the style of his coat or the cut of his hair, but these are unimportant compared with the feeling the boy has inside him. The time will soon come when he will be more like the parents he is fighting now than any other persons in his life. When he feels confident in his ability to handle himself, he will return to the ideal of an adult he has developed over the years.

Adults can prepare themselves and the boy for his acquaintance and at-homeness with girls. Perhaps the emphasis for adults can be more properly placed on preparing themselves for the boy's dating than on preparing the boy, for at this stage the boy will follow the pattern of the group. The attitude, however, that the boy will carry to these first relationships with girls will be the one he formed in early childhood with his mother.

Some adults push a boy toward dating and some tend to hold him back. Neither pattern will be very helpful. When the boy enters adolescence, he will be physiologically preparing for interest in the opposite sex. How fast he moves in that direction will depend in large part on the satisfaction he and members of his group have in their first relationships. A boy's first date, which should be on his own initiative, will probably be one of the most memorable events of his adolescence. Most parents will welcome this interest, not only because it indicates that his emotional growth is advancing but because, if successful, it will make him feel more able to be on his own, and more adult. It will mark a new phase of social adaptation and development in his life.

Unfortunately some of these dating days are often slow and painful. Boys feel unsure of themselves. Embarrassment or failure is hard to swallow, and they do not know what girls expect of them. This is where the group can be a big aid. They often bring in a panel of girls to discuss these questions or they use films that suggest the more effective ways to handle oneself. Some clubs have invited an older girl whom they respect, sometimes an older sister of a club member, to answer their questions, and have gained real confidence without embarrassment.

A junior high school poll of five hundred girls listed the following ten qualities as the most desirable in boys:

1. manners
2. friendliness
3. appearance
4. sense of humor
5. good sport
6. good talker
7. liked by other boys
8. fond of dancing
9. liked by other girls
10. the crowd to which he belongs

Most first dates are group dates, either club parties or with members of the club. Adults can be of great help in planning these parties, but they should not make the mistake of planning without the boys themselves. Boys and girls can have wonderful times together as a group of young people, sometimes pairing off, sometimes not. Activities which can be conducted as a group are more helpful at this age than those requiring couples. This helps the group member who is somewhat flustered in the company of one girl to get some understanding of what is expected of him when the coupling-off time comes. Small group activities, such as parties at someone's house, picnics, beach parties, skating, hiking, bicycling, swimming, are lots of fun.

Adults can provide or guide the boy toward adequate sex information. Sex instruction is not something that parents can introduce to the boy for the first time at this age. Long before now he has decided whether or not the family is a source of adequate information. Parents can still stimulate questions and give frank answers, but they will not be able to supply all the information the boy seeks at this time.

Adults should know that the majority of boys play with their genitals during this period. It is another expression of their self-interest and their centering of attention on themselves. Masturbation is seldom discussed between the generations because of unnecessary anxiety on the part of adults or shame on the part of the boy. This type of sex play usually diminishes as the boy achieves a sense of independence and is able to direct his attention outward toward other activities and interests.

It is clear now that information and understanding of one's

body is an essential part of the growth of respect for one's body and a healthy outlook on life. Within the group, there is an excellent opportunity for fathers and sons to share in discussions led by men with accurate knowledge. Feelings about sex should be discussed as well as the physiological facts. If fathers and sons attend together, they may ask questions of each other more easily after the meeting. If boys do not want their fathers present, it is best that they meet alone with their adult leader and the speaker. Excellent films and books are available to supplement these discussions.

The more boys understand about their bodies, the more pride they will develop in them. Regular physical examinations by the family or team physician give them opportunities to ask questions of others. Boys who come from families where sex is accepted as a normal part of life and respect for the body and each other is practiced, will make their adjustment to puberty more easily than boys from homes where sex is taboo. Sex stories need not be encouraged, but it should be understood that they often help adolescents laugh about something that has been frightening to them.

Adults can help boys increase their acquaintance and experience with the world. This is a place where adults can be of direct help. Any contact a boy of this age can have with his world is helpful, especially as it relates to the task that men have in it. This can include trips, talks with visual aids, discussions, movies, but above all, firsthand information where they see the world at work. The closer they can get to knowing and seeing the men who are doing the work, the better the experience. The fathers of the boys in a group, or any fathers in a community, can arrange these experiences for their sons. Of course, a boy will usually want his friend to go along.

Adults can help boys become more articulate about their philosophy of life. Throughout this chapter, emphasis has been placed on group contacts and contacts with individual men. Boys of this age should have contacts with many friendly adults, and opportunities are many for these men to reveal the values by which they guide their lives. These need not be preachy or elaborate statements. In fact, it is better if they are not. A question by someone who cares may cause another to reveal a truth that the boy of this age finds difficult to accept from his father. The family dinner, where members tell of their day's experiences, presents opportunities to ask questions that make values stand out clearly. Incidents in every daily paper provide situations where family judgment can be sought. A habit of evaluating life and an atmosphere where movements of high inspiration can be revealed build toward a philosophy of life. Conferences of youth under religious organizational sponsorship and leadership are most helpful in this regard.

During all of this period, understanding parents remain relaxed most of the time, yet cling firmly but quietly to a few essentials. They talk to their boy when he is relaxed and able to listen. These are the times when he can best understand. These parents are not surprised that their son has not become completely civilized by the time he is fourteen. They know it takes time to grow a personality.

CHAPTER 16

How a Boy Develops in Middle Adolescence (Ages 15-16-17)

Prelude

This is the star boarder who comes home for meals and needs a private secretary to keep straight his game schedules and appointments. He seldom allows homework to interfere with his pleasures and even when he looks at a book, he may be dreaming of a blonde or trying to work out a new play for the team. Parents, of course, still don't understand him. They are just as old-fashioned as they were when he was twelve. It is rather a nuisance for adolescents to try to bring up their parents as well as solve the problems of the world—and get very far with either job.

The world of middle adolescence

The world of middle adolescence is still a welter of conflicts —all the conflicts of early adolescence intensified, on a higher level, one step nearer resolution. It is a world in which a youth sees people staring questioningly at him at every turn, more than ever demanding that he be independent, adequate, competent, and at the same time that he be loving. They seem to be asking what kind of a man he is, or thinks he is, or can be now that he is a person apart from his family. Few of these eyes seem sympathetic.

His contemporaries view him suspiciously if he is not loyal to his group and free from his family. They are taking the measure of his independence and his adequacy by their standards. If they smile and give him a nod, he is "in" and happy. If they just stare at him, it is because he has not grown up enough for them. If they turn their gaze away altogether, it is because they feel he is hopeless; then he is beset by social fears and he resorts to bizarre and sometimes dangerous behavior to convince himself and them that he is worthy of their approval.

His family's eyes have a touch of sympathy and understanding, but even they may reveal a trace of dismay and hurt and bewilderment. How can they see life as he does, keep apace with his shifting feelings and moods and confusions? At their best, they are striving to understand and accept this new person who is their son. At their worst, they wonder what has come over him to make him act so queerly; they feel it is time for this nonsense to end. To the boy, they seem to be threatening him with more new restraints that thwart his path to manhood; to retaliate self-defensively, he will blame them for things not at all their fault. Actually he wants to find trust and love and understanding in his parents' eyes because he secretly still admires their strength and wisdom, and relies on them as an ever-present refuge.

The adults in the community seem to expect an answer, too. They have paid taxes to provide him an education and they have sacrificed to build a fine community for him to grow up in; now it is up to him to prove that their efforts have not been in vain. Their eyes seem to demand some evidence of his competence—a competence he wants as much as they.

Within this encirclement of eyes, he sees only one kind that is not completely critical. Their beauty is becoming steadily more impelling to him. They offer a companionship if he, with masculine initiative, will take the first step. If others were not watching, he would probably rush to her to answer the new, insistent inner drive toward feminine friendships—and to escape the others. But they are watching him; and with every move he makes, the ideas of "adequacy" and "competence" arise to plague him. He wants to master all the amenities that will improve his standing among girls, and make him feel at ease with them. He is enthusiastic about new pursuits that lead to social activities. Partly attributable to this drive is his greater interest in earning money, in excelling in sports, in dressing according to his peers' latest vogue, and in the serious matter of planning toward higher education, a vocation, and a family.

Generally, a sports event is now enjoyed more as spectator rather than participant, though interest may increase in long-term sports such as tennis, golf, skiing, and swimming.

You may be surprised any day to find the youth tinkering with the family radio, TV set, or car. Or if he's old enough by his state's laws to drive, he will be repairing or painting his garish jalopy—still one more item on his agenda for success with girls, and another (sometimes hazardous) means of satisfying his craving for excitement and adventure. Most of his mechanical interests, however, begin to narrow down, to specialize. He may become, for example, one of the school's electronic experts, but may find woodworking boring.

His rapidly developing reasoning powers, ability to make judgments, attention span, and learning ability combine with his heightened need for status to increase his love of discussion and argument—particularly in resisting the adult world. Though tending to be more individual and specialized in interest, his reading habits are practically those of an adult. He may begin to parade opinions and knowledge as yet another way to impress his feminine audience.

His intellectual questing, propitious for the formation of a well-reasoned philosophy of life and code of ethics, may lead him temporarily to religious skepticism. Later he discovers that the values he holds are much like those of adults. Then he becomes conservative and never wants those values to change.

A youth's idealism runs high at this period, unperturbed by adult pessimism or "realism." He identifies easily with the troubled or the courageous. He wants genuinely to be of service. His sense of justice is keen; breakdowns in society puzzle him —yet racial or religious prejudice may seem "natural" to him if his group or family has inculcated it. He may attach himself to a group that is snobbish and excludes some of his contemporaries who do not meet the group's special standards of popularity, skill, economic status, or racial, religious, or national background. This is twofold evidence of inadequate democratic training and present feelings of insecurity. To belong to themselves, to exclude others, makes them feel stronger and superior, possessing especially meritorious attributes.

A youth looks to someone for confirmation or denial of his ideas, to almost anyone beyond his home. He respects those whom he can reject or accept as he wishes. He will often work wholeheartedly with the voluntarily accepted adult if he has a share in the planning; at other times, he may take advantage of the friendship.

He is moving close to manhood. He often begins to feel adequate and self-assured, and always wants to feel that way. He wants to be taken as a man able to handle his own affairs. He is often highly critical of himself. The times when he is the most noisy and the most cocky are usually the times when he is least sure of himself. He is deeply concerned about his status with his peers—and with society as a whole. These fears are social; he fears that he may not be able to identify himself with society as a self-sufficient individual. He does not want to stand alone.

Becoming an adult can be a frightening adventure.

Developmental tasks of middle adolescence

In middle adolescence, the tasks needing most attention, those most crucial if the youth is to attain stature as a worthy person, separate and distinct from his family, are those which increase his sense of adequacy and competence.

There are giant strides to be taken, but none of them is completely new. Each is a continuation of a task started earlier in life. Each is taking a form which requires him to appear more and more like an adult. These tasks will not reach their final form in middle adolescence, but they should be well started. The years of late adolescence will still be devoted to some of these same tasks—and a few continue throughout life, though on a higher meaning level. Despite this extended time, however, the middle adolescent should be proceeding successfully with these tasks. Those youths who are most advanced will appear most stable.

In the listings and descriptions of the tasks which follow, it will be noted that an asterisk (*) appears before each numeral —which indicates that all of these tasks are deemed to be major ones.

*1. *Feeling equal to becoming an adult.* The boy in middle adolescence must discard finally and completely his image of childhood and see himself becoming a young man, an emerging adult, and he must feel equal to this role toward which he is reaching and which is expected of him. Most of his confidence will rest on his feelings about how well he has handled life up till now. If he has had more successes than failures in his relations with his contemporaries, if he has been able to move toward handling his own life without feelings of self-abasement, and if he has come to accept his own body and his sex role without too much anxiety, he will take this step in stride. These are the times where he needs unobtrusive support if he seems to hesitate. Competence in any field can lend a feeling of success that will encourage acceptance by his contemporaries; but it will not substitute for a healthy self-image of himself as an emerging man. He must identify himself as an emerging adult in order to feel equal to the task. He must lose much of his self-centering and be able to join with others in new ideas, new causes, and new relationships. He needs to realize the new self-acceptance that brings a kind of inner peace and enables him to end the war within himself, to become truly a part of the culture and world in which he lives. Then he can move toward considering the well-being of others.

*2. *Being able to attract the one he desires—being able to give and receive love.* The boy in middle adolescence now has a compelling need to be able to win his way with girls. He needs to know how to attract those who seem most desirable. If any of the early stages of acquaintance or courtship are undeveloped, he needs help quickly so that he will be able to conduct himself with ease. He needs broad social experience so that he may know many girls and participate in a variety of co-ed activities. He needs to be able to discriminate between superficial feminine allure and enduring feminine qualities. As girls begin to become young women in his eyes, he needs more help in understanding the obligations that go with courtship and engagement. As he approaches late adolescence, he needs sound information on marriage and family life.

*3. *Achieving a working relationship with his family which permits considerable freedom, yet retains understanding and affection.* The boy in middle adolescence needs to know what he can expect of his family. He wants to gain more control of his life without hurting them. He needs to feel that he is loved and wanted, but does not want this to hamper his independence. He wants to be treated more as a partner than as a dependent child. He feels his ideas can contribute to the family, too.

As at any age, the adolescent needs a stable home, one where living is so consistent that he can predict quite accurately what its attitude will be toward his behavior. He needs to know that his attitudes toward his home and family are fairly normal so that they are not accompanied by feelings of guilt.

He needs a chance to share planning with all the family. This planning includes the responsibilities and privileges in the home as well as a consideration of the behavior of the members. The family council or some other conference plan works well in the democratic home. It fails when it is dominated by either parents or youth. In these cases, adults can expect revolt. The adolescent cannot submit to parental authority and become independent. He is usually ready for more responsibility than adults are willing to place in his hands. He still needs a clear picture of what independence really is. He tends to see the freedoms of adults without their responsibilities. He experiments, sometimes adopts adult behavior, such as smoking, drinking, and staying out late, to support his need to feel adult and independent.

*4. *Achieving a close friendship with some others like himself.* The boy in middle adolescence must be able to win approval from the crowd of his own age. His primary fear is fear of isolation. He must have somebody to talk with, someone to stand around with him. Within this crowd he needs to find friends. In early adolescence the crowd was enough, but now he requires more intimate, deep association with a few who can share his social, emotional, and intellectual experiences. He needs these intimate friends to assess his standing in the adolescent culture.

This growing need for intimate friends does not replace his need for membership in some purposeful group of his contemporaries. This purposeful group, however, should not end with its identity within itself. It should provide the doorway to association with other similar groups within his community and country. This larger association will provide opportunities for new friends and a wider checking of his values. It will develop wider loyalties and a larger social consciousness.

*5. *Understanding sex as a creative force and achieving outlets consistent with his ideals.* The boy in middle adolescence needs a positive view of sex. He needs an understanding of sex far beyond the proper names of the sex organs or an understanding of biological functioning. These are prerequisites, but now he needs an understanding of his feelings. He thrills to these new erotic feelings and observations but needs help in organizing his thoughts about himself and his emotions.

He needs to see these experiences in relation to the culture in which he lives as well as to the family he plans to have. He needs to see sex not as a plaything but as a creative force entirely consistent with his highest ideals. He needs to know how one manages sex feelings in our day with its extended education and its high economic demands. Before he can discuss the subject freely, he needs to know that sex feelings are normal and are not to be feared; that sex has a place in life. He can acquire this knowledge only with a background of accurate information and free discussion.

*6. *Accepting his body with its strengths and weaknesses and feeling able to contribute to life with it.* The boy in middle adolescence needs to arrive at a state where he accepts his body for what it is, whether his attitude toward his body is one of pride or one of tolerance. Along with this acceptance of his body, he needs to accept his masculine role. He is greatly aided in doing both of these if his body size and power cause others to see him as a man. To be undeveloped physically, sickly, overweight, pimply, or to vary otherwise from the body form that gains quick acceptance is a cross to bear for most adolescents. Until he has won recognition from others of his own age for some skill or leadership, he will probably find it difficult to accept or become tolerant of his body. If his associates accept him, his role as a man is assured.

Success in sports means acceptance of his body; failure in sports raises doubts about his body. He needs to be helped in the selection of a sport where he has the greatest chance of success. He also needs to be guided to the level of competition appropriate to his potential. If his body will not sustain him in competitive sports, he should be encouraged in related activities, such as sports writing or photography or team management, or directed to some other field of endeavor where his inadequacy will not plague him or threaten his self-esteem.

On the normal assumption that girls are not attracted to

effeminate boys, he needs feminine social acceptance to achieve his own acceptance of his body.

*7. *Accepting and meeting society's demand for competence.* The boy in middle adolescence needs opportunities for achievements that win recognition from the adult world around him. He has an increasing desire to achieve as a means of demonstrating to himself and those about him that he has worth; he needs the self-respect that comes from being of worth, of having skills that are of value, of making a significant contribution to social living now. He seeks the rewards of social prestige and needs chances to live creatively. He needs to see the results of his efforts and to know they are good.

The boy in middle adolescence is as highly critical of himself as he is of almost everyone else. He needs assurance that he can make good, needs the opportunity of understanding himself, as gained through the life of a group and sharing in some of the emotional experiences of others. He needs help in working out ways of handling his aggressive feelings through an interest in and an appreciation of other persons in the group. He needs to accept responsibility within a group and to work with them on their common problems rather than cling to the fear of losing his individuality.

*8. *Having some identification of his place in the world's work and having a positive attitude toward work.* The boy in middle adolescence feels society's pressure on him to profit from all they have provided and become a self-respecting, economic unit. He also wonders where he can contribute enough to achieve economic independence. The longer his vocational choice is undecided or puzzling to him, the higher the tension grows and the more difficult it is for him to be prepared. Even though his vocational choices may change often, the adolescent who thinks he knows what he wants to do finds it easier to make adjustments in daily living. He needs opportunities for vocational practice. He needs the discipline and experience of work. He needs an opportunity to earn money and to spend and save it wisely.

*9. *Being able to use leisure time creatively.* The boy in middle adolescence needs the opportunity to choose his leisure-time activities and to enjoy them with his friends rather than with the family. In leisure time he can most truly be himself and discover the kind of person he is. Since this self-discovery is one of his major tasks, leisure time is especially important to him.

He needs opportunities to share in leisure-time planning and creating. He needs the entire range from light, social frivolity to deep commitment to a great cause. He needs muscular as well as mental stimulus. He needs to test himself in activities with others like himself. He needs hobbies, skill in popular games, and acquaintance with his culture to make wise use of his leisure time.

*10. *Being able and willing to apply religious values to his own life and situation.* The boy in middle adolescence must have some faith on which he can depend and around which he can organize his life. Religion provides this core. It provides a meaningful answer to the universe and a worthy place for each individual. It provides a pattern for his ideal self; yet if he falls short, it sustains him when he comprehends an understanding and forgiving God. A religious faith which thus inspires and challenges, but does not condemn or reject, will provide the sense of identity and integration that the adolescent needs.

The boy in middle adolescence needs chances to participate in religion-based discussions of the problems that he faces personally and the problems faced by his group and their ever growing community.

He needs to appreciate the struggle behind mankind's achievements so that he can understand the dynamic motivations of religion. He needs contact with friendly adults whose lives reveal the purpose and friendliness of the universe. His philosophy must grow in harmony with both scientific and spiritual values.

Major responsibilities of adults with boys in middle adolescence

Middle adolescence is a trying time for adults who want to help youth. The needs appear greater and greater, but the separation between the generations seems to be getting wider and wider. Those in our culture who bear the greatest responsibility in guiding boys at this age—parents and teachers—are usually the most rejected. How *can* adults co-operate with them effectively?

The answer has been given by teen-agers in both action and words countless times, but it bears repeating. Here it is, in youth's own words: "We want you to believe in us, just for ourselves. We want to be better just as you want us to be better, but we can win more easily if you take us as we are and believe in us. We think you're grand when you can laugh with us and make us feel that 'kids are fun.' We'll respond to your touch and guidance then. It's sorta—well, easy does it."

How could it be otherwise? For this is the period when the youth's main task is to become an independent, self-directing person. He is not seeking a rejection of adults as much as he is seeking a new acceptance of himself. He is on the road of high adventure. Adults who want to help will support him in his endeavors, but through more indirect action than before. He will rebel against those who try overtly to exert control over his life. The adult he can reject or not as he wishes wins his respect and confidence and co-operation. Any adult whose attitudes toward young people parallels those of the model adult—described by the teen-agers quoted above—is in an enviably strong position to contribute to their growth. Any adult who gives adolescents the impression that they are children can expect to be rejected. It would be unhealthy if he were not.

Adults who want to contribute to youth will need to listen to youth. Adults cannot possibly know how a youth feels until he tells them. Experiences of their own youth are not a reliable guide; even if they were, it is hard for an adolescent to picture adults as being up-to-date. When parents shift from "When I was a boy . . ." to "What is your crowd doing?" they are beginning to understand their adolescent.

Adults can support boys in their striving toward independence and identity. The adolescent needs and welcomes the approval of adults in relation to what he is trying to accomplish. At this period of life when he is often not too clear himself as to what he is trying to do, praise of adults for efforts to stand on his own feet meets a directional need as well as an emotional hunger.

A group of older adolescents recently classified their parents as "egg beaters" or "good eggs." "You are an egg beater," they said, "when there is no way of avoiding the steady nagging that eventually beats us into a froth. Most of you don't know what you are doing because you cover it with a pose of interest in us. We can't see how it can be much fun to want to rule the roost if it just chases us all away. We would appreciate a little less interest in perfection and a little more acquaintance with us as we really are."

"You're a good egg," they declared, "when you realize the hatching season is over and you don't try to sit on us all the time. Somehow we believe home is a place to enjoy and love each other. It is a place where people are tied by love, not by apron strings. Tie us to you and we will struggle to be free. Love us and let us try our own wings and we will snuggle close to you when we get hurt."

A delicate balance must be maintained between letting adolescents be on their own and at the same time not giving them more responsibility than they are prepared to handle. Although they need the counsel of adults, they also need to be free to experience making their own decisions. They need enough freedom of decision to be able to make mistakes, but not the kind of mistakes that harm others or mar their estimate of themselves. On the other hand, giving them too much freedom does not aid their independence; it adds to their confusion. Some youths need to be encouraged, some need to be challenged, but the pace or the type of guidance comes from the boy himself.

Adolescents should continue to carry responsibilities around the home and they will do so without undue pressure if parents support them in their desire for independence. This depends mostly upon the method of planning. If they share in distributing the family responsibilities and can have reasonable freedom in carrying out those responsibilities assigned to them, they will do their best work.

Parents should involve the boy in the sharing and solving of inevitable family problems. The real test of family living is not the presence of problems but how the family meets them. The boy's own maturation and his respect for the home—its members and their values—will be strengthened by such experiences. This may require more listening by the parent than usually occurs.

Parents' efforts to help young people solve their difficult problems will be misunderstood less frequently if the problems are discussed frankly and calmly around the family table. When the adolescent's feelings are deeply involved, the discussion should be postponed tactfully until a more opportune moment arrives. Minor problems should not be tackled in family councils but should be resolved by the boy himself.

Parents should largely ignore the aggressiveness of adolescents. To return the aggressiveness impatiently, heightens tensions and can embitter the adolescent. During his struggle to find himself and to achieve independence, the adolescent very commonly belittles his parents. He seems to become angriest at those he loves best. Most parents expect their relationship with their boy to change during adolescence; but few are fully prepared for the dismaying discovery that they are being not only rejected but attacked as well. It is far easier to absorb the blow when parents recognize this behavior as further evidence that their son is growing up, that he is really using them as a ready target for his dissatisfaction with his own progress.

Adults can co-operate with boys in their group life. Most of the worries that keep teen-agers awake in troubled nights arise from their social relationships with others of their own age. An adolescent who has many friends and many interests has the better chance of developing a happy design for living. Wise parents will encourage their son in these associations, especially when the boys are engaging in some purposeful program with the assistance of friendly adults. Often other boys can do more with an adolescent than the boy's father can, even though the father be well informed or well adjusted.

All during their son's childhood and adolescence, the parents have been anxious to have him reflect credit on them. Now the tables are turned and the middle adolescent is anxious lest they bring discredit on him. This means that parents as individuals will find it very difficult to co-operate with a son in a club; but groups of parents have found significant ways to enrich the life of these clubs.

As in early adolescence, parent co-operation depends largely upon their treatment of the boys as equals. The parents of the boys in the group should make plans in the light of the boys' needs, in counsel with their adviser and any organization involved. These plans should then be presented to the group as an invitation which the group is free to accept or reject. If there are no strings attached, the group usually receives the invitation favorably, as a recognition of their worth and independence.

Parents who have achieved this kind of partnership with a group find these extremely happy occasions. The boys are sufficiently mature to be very companionable, and these associations together prove inspiring to adults and youth alike. Some of the co-operation will be at the times and in the ways suggested by the group itself. Adult acceptance of these opportunities opens the way for more activities together.

Most of the sharing by adults will be in situations where boys outnumber adults. A father, speaking to the group as he would to his own son, is welcomed by the group. Strange as it seems, most boys indicate that they want more advice than they get. They seem to want it most in these informal settings where they are free to discuss it and to accept or reject it as they wish. Talks on high school, athletics, vocations, college, religion, and the armed services are popular. A youth finds it easier to accept the ideas of these guests than the ideas of his own parents. He finds them of inestimable value in shaping his own life.

Adults often get other requests to participate in programs where the boys take the lead and do the planning. These may be such club programs as inductions, town hall meetings, dinners, or events needing financial support. Girls will be involved in some of the activities; adults will be needed to help in many of these co-ed projects.

Adults can trust boys in their dating adventures. For a boy, dating involves a highly technical procedure where his behavior is being critically rated by his peers. It involves tension, frustration, anxiety, and many other emotions before he will arrive at the time when he selects the one to share his life.

He participates in parties, dances, outings, sports, and many school experiences in the company of girls. He exchanges gifts and physical expressions of affection and respect that accompany this experience. He wants to spend more and more time in the company of girls, sometimes at the expense of school work. Hours of returning home get later. Allowances become greater. Adults know less and less about his activities.

It is easy to see how adult worries can mount. A mother sometimes feels that no girl is good enough for her son, and a father feels no boy is qualified to protect his daughter. Their parents probably felt the same way. There's another way to look at it, however. The task for adults is to help make this new experience contribute the most to their son and to those who share dating with him. There are enough heartaches and headaches in it as it is without adults adding more. How can this be done?

Dating time should be welcomed when it comes. The average boy has participated in school parties, "gang dates," and some dates on his own by fourteen or fifteen years and will be ready for more frequent dating by sixteen or seventeen years. It comes when he is ready for it and it cannot be forced.

Adults should know where and with whom he is spending his time. It need not be a detailed outline which limits his freedom or makes him feel anxious if he must co-operate with the crowd, but it should include a who, where, and when. Adolescents enjoy being out at night. It is not only exciting but adult. Hours will pass quickly. He will need to have some plan by which to guide his hours. It is better if this is not a set hour, for occasions differ. The plan will need to consider his responsibilities, his health, the group pattern. Understandings are better than rules.

He will need help in seeing his responsibility to others. Explanations need not be preachy but can appeal to his sense of fair play. These are days when his experience with his home and his self-image will guide him. It is the time to believe in him, to expect that the pattern of life he has established through his association with adults is adequate. It is too late for any other procedure.

Adults can provide opportunities for boys to relieve sex anxieties. The changed cultural concepts regarding sex behavior and the weakening of the old codes place greater responsibility on a boy than ever before. He needs to understand that fulfillment of love lies far beyond any sexual experimentation motivated by anxieties about his normalcy, his masculinity. His anxieties about ever being loved, about how to express his love, about having sex desires and thoughts, cannot be met by ignorance. These feelings are too strong to be mastered by a ghost. Boys and girls alike need this vital information if they are to respect each other's integrity. Greater freedom to understand and discuss sex is not designed to bring lesser but greater responsibility on the part of the individual.

Few parents will be able to answer all their son's questions adequately. But they can take advantage of the ideal setting for presenting and discussing this information expertly—organization and club meetings—where qualified specialists can answer questions accurately and far more objectively. Many religious leaders specializing in this area and many religiously oriented doctors are available in most communities to give such help.

Adults can help boys find their place in the world's work. An adolescent needs to assure himself of his worth to the world by finding a place in its economy. Adults expect him to show an adult interest in the world's work but seldom give him a chance to share significantly in it. In times of war, a youth finds it easy to secure adult vocational status; in times of peace, he is often in competition with adults.

In primitive societies, ceremonials marked certain stages of growth. Following these ceremonials, a youth carried a more responsible role in the tribe. Adult society today provides very few of these ceremonials. The world of work provides the most significant step by which he moves into adult society.

Since the family has delegated more and more of its economic functions to the community, an adolescent finds it necessary to move into the community to carry this responsibility. Child labor laws may delay him in achieving significant work experience if his vocational choice does not involve higher education. Society expects him to make good in the world's work, yet in such a case it tends to thwart him. Society seems to be aware of this and though it still places high value upon economic achievement, it is too often satisfied if the youth makes progress in selecting his field of work and can tell adults what he plans to do. Society seldom follows up to see how few really can do what they had hoped to do.

Many youths drop out of school, seeking some measure of financial independence and the coveted status of an adult. Few are prepared for the difficulties they will encounter. Those who hope to work after high school are at a disadvantage in competing with adults and often have an unsatisfactory introduction to the world's work. They do not know the kinds of work they can perform successfully. They do not know their own abilities or the jobs that are open to them. Few understand what will be expected of them, and many do not understand how to co-operate with other workers.

Work outside the home, while still in school, can provide an adolescent with some understanding of the work of the world. A youth needs the vocational counsel of adults to get a good start in the working world. Trips to industry, talks with personnel men, and contacts with employers can help a youth in his vocational choice and prepare him for the world's work. These work experiences should not be left to chance. They should provide vocational exploration. They must not use more of his growing energy than he can spare. Scholarship information, vocational testing, and the school-work program provide more opportunities for the adults who care about a youth's adjustment to the world's work.

Adults can help boys find meaning in life. Boys in middle adolescence need contact with men with power and poise in the world, who seem to have found meaning in life beyond their jobs. They have found a oneness with the universe and their daily work is related to this cause. Because of this ultimate meaning, they are not alone. They have found the way to meet situations that require courage above their own powers; they enjoy a fellowship with God.

Adults can also help adolescents realize the basic need for good will between himself and his fellow men. Love is a spiritual need of man. Within this spiritual relationship, man has status as a child of God, and all his fellow men become brothers. This becomes the core of life around which man organizes his values. Destiny lies within this realm and boys will respond to life on this high purpose. What a boy needs desperately is intimate contact with someone who can so interpret these religious values that he can see life in these greater meanings.

Adults can encourage the middle adolescent in the feeling that he can meet life successfully and that adults will always stand by to help if the going gets rough. Parents start training their son when he is a baby, toward the day when he will stand

BASIC TASKS	EARLY CHILDHOOD 3 - 4 - 5 YEARS	MIDDLE CHILDHOOD 6 - 7 - 8 YEARS About Grades 1-2-3
1. Developing a self-image he can respect	Accepting himself as a separate, distinct individual of worth	Feeling accepted by the person (or persons) in his intimate world who exemplify the ideal way of acting to him
2. Developing a pattern of affection	Having ability to show affection toward others	Having ability to share affection
3. Achieving independence and self management	Developing a sense of physical independence within a framework of dependence	Reaching toward independence
4. Relating one's self to his social group	Enjoying play in the company of others	Enjoying play with a friend
5. Learning one's sex role	Becoming aware of sex differences and adjusting to cultural pattern of sex differences	Identifying with a masculine role
6. Accepting one's body	Growing—continuing big muscle development and motor abilities	Developing finer muscle control and motor abilities
7. Accepting society's demand for competence	Developing elementary cultural patterns of physical care	Feeling successful in his efforts
8. Finding one's place in work	Developing initiative and language communication	Doing small tasks under his own power and direction
9. Finding adventure and joy in living	Extending his acquaintance with his environment	Increasing his acquaintance with his environment
10. Developing a value system	Accepting controls from others—beginning of some self control from a developing conscience	Increasing his ability to take directions from others and direct himself from within

LATE CHILDHOOD 9 - 10 - 11 YEARS About Grades 4-5-6	EARLY ADOLESCENCE 12 - 13 - 14 YEARS About Grades 7-8-9	MIDDLE ADOLESCENCE 15 - 16 - 17 YEARS About Grades 10-11-12
Feeling accepted and effective as a member of his own age and sex contemporaries	Feeling wanted by his contemporaries and feeling able to contribute to them	Feeling equal to becoming an adult
Beginning to find joy in making others happy	Developing an acquaintance and at-homeness with girls—feeling worthy of love	Being able to attract the one he admires—to give and receive love
Responding to the group, yet feeling he can rely upon his home	Being eager and increasingly able to direct his own life	Achieving a working relationship with the family, permitting considerable freedom, yet retaining understanding and affection.
Winning his way with a group	Winning and holding membership in an intimate group of his own age and sex	Achieving a close friendship with some others like himself
Accepting a masculine role in his group life	Understanding his body and developing positive attitudes toward sex life	Understanding sex as a creative force and achieving outlets consistent with his ideals
Being confident of his ability to grow up	Feeling confident that he is normal	Accepting his body with its strengths and weaknesses and feeling able to contribute to life with it.
Feeling useful to someone or something	Feeling of value to some group or cause	Accepting and meeting society's demand for competence
Increasing his acquaintance with the adult world	Increasing his experience with the world in which he lives	Having some identification of his place in the world's work and a positive attitude toward work
Daring to express his feeling for adventure	Finding joy in the active use of his body and mind	Being able to use leisure time creatively
Increasing his interest in fair play and justice	Becoming articulate about some philosophy of life	Being able and willing to apply religious values to his own life and situations

on his own feet and be a person in his own right. Now that this day has arrived they should be glad and enjoy life with him. He's probably going to be everything they dared to hope if they will keep on believing in him.

CHAPTER 17

A Boy and His Parents Today

Living together

The task at hand, then—as outlined in this book—is living, loving, and learning together with the boy in his childhood days; and living, respecting, and co-operating with him as he struggles through his adolescence toward adulthood. This brings inspiring days and days of deep inner anxiety for both the boy and the adult, but where is the generation who would give up its children to avoid these anxieties? Living together is not always easy. The going is often rough. It is rough for the boy as well as for the adult. The greatest growth usually occurs at these very points of stress. Resistance is often the means for new creative living. The boy, however, has the right to expect that this resistance is based upon understanding and not upon blocks that confuse the issue. This book has sought to give the kind of understanding that makes living together easier—and often fun.

The boy has been seen, not as a small adult, but as a person who is growing toward adulthood. He lives in the world as it appears to him, pressured by forces from within, from his culture, and from his contemporaries. At times he interprets this world as the adults do, and his behavior is satisfactory. At other times he interprets this world differently than adults do, but he can act only in response to the world he sees. His behavior is always normal to him.

The boy gets his basic outlook on life within his home. From the feeling of love and worth he experiences, he builds a self-image which influences him throughout life. He moves out from this home into the larger community and seeks to establish himself as competent and adequate to be an adult.

As he grows, he passes through definite stages, at which times his growth and his culture place specific tasks before him for mastery. These tasks come to him progressively as developmental tasks, and the adults who are near him can provide opportunities through which these tasks can be accomplished.

The major task of adults is to be on the boy's side, trying to understand what he is trying to do and helping him to win. They will permit him to set the pace of his own growth—getting the cue from him—encouraging or challenging him according to his need. They expect that he will make some mistakes, but these will provide opportunities for new learning rather than censure and new prohibitions.

Fortunate indeed is the boy born into today's world. True, a boy is born into the atomic world, the "age of anxiety." But he is born into a world where man's understanding of man—in psychology, psychiatry, social psychology, all social sciences—has reached its greatest height, as has man's scientific understanding of his universe.

True, a boy is born into a complex world to which he must make even more and greater adjustments than his father. But he will have access, thanks to this same complex culture, to an even greater number of more powerful tools with which to control his world.

True, a boy is born into a world of conflict, oppression, and war. But he is also born into a family more democratic than ever before in man's history; he is born into a community expanding its services, both publicly and privately sponsored, and extending them democratically to greater numbers of boys of all classes, creeds, colors, and national origins; he is born into a country where democracy is still very much alive; he is born into a world where, despite heartbreaking setbacks, mankind is struggling forward daily toward the light of freedom everywhere.

Fortunate indeed are the parents of a boy born into today's world. They no longer feel inhibited—as did their parents perhaps—in giving their son their unstinted love; they know that love is no longer "old-fashioned," but strongly buttressed by scientific knowledge; they know their boy cannot have too much love at any age, so long as their love is shared equally among all members of the family.

Parents today find their son a perpetual challenge to them—a creative and rejuvenating challenge. Every phase of his development—physical, mental, social, and emotional—is at a quickened pace. He enters adolescence a little earlier and tends to grow taller than his father and grandfather. Our accumulated knowledge and our advanced means of communicating it by radio and TV thrust into his mind facts of which parents often are yet unaware; his questioning at every age is more perplexing than ever to conscientious parents who want to give honest and intelligent answers, or guide their boy to the sources of those answers. A boy is propelled into the community earlier and into a greater number of activities than ever before; parents find that in order to keep contact with their boy, they must enter into the community life as never before. A boy's greater social freedom in adolescence is profoundly more influential in forcing him to accept responsibilities from which parents would have sheltered him a generation or two ago; his parents are challenged daily to let—and help—their son achieve that responsibility, which is at once mental, social, and emotional.

Parents are fortunate too because they are better prepared

than in any previous generation to love and understand their son, and to guide him patiently and intelligently toward successful manhood. It is a far cry indeed from the pioneering days of G. Stanley Hall. Our knowledge of a boy's development is now widespread—and the seeking out for that knowledge even more widespread than before. Qualified consultants are available in every community, among specially trained school teachers, clergymen, and youth leaders and counselors in public and private service agencies. Libraries everywhere are increasing their resources of child guidance books, as both supply and demand increase in quality and quantity.

Parents and their sons today have every reason to celebrate each day they share together, for they are living in a world potentially the greatest mankind has ever known—in love and understanding, in social, spiritual, and technological progress, and in the promise for the future.

Sources for More Information

Each of these leading national organizations serving child and family life have complete publication lists which will be sent on request. These publications are up to date and the cost is nominal.

American Association for Health, Physical Education and Recreation, 1201 16th St., N. W., Washington 6, D. C.

American Medical Association, 555 North Dearborn St., Chicago 10, Ill.

American Social Hygiene Association, 1790 Broadway, New York 19, N. Y.

Association for Childhood Education International, 1200 15th St., N. W., Washington 5, D. C.

Child Study Association of America, 132 East 74th St., New York 21, N. Y.

Children's Bureau, Department of Health, Education, and Welfare, Washington 25, D. C.

Family Service Association of America, 192 Lexington Ave., New York 16, N. Y.

National Committee for Mental Hygiene, 1790 Broadway, New York 19, N. Y.

National Congress of Parents and Teachers, 600 South Michigan Blvd., Chicago 5, Ill.

National Council on Family Relations, 5757 South Drexel Ave., Chicago 37, Ill.

Public Affairs Committee, Inc., 22 East 38th St., New York 16, N. Y.

Science Research Associates, 57 West Grand Ave., Chicago 10, Ill.

Y.M.C.A., Association Press, 291 Broadway, New York 7, N. Y.

The public library in your community has excellent books, magazines, and pamphlet materials on family and child life. The librarian will gladly help you find them.